TIME OFF
IN SCOTLAND

Cover designed by Raymond Hawkey

Other titles in this series

TIME OFF
IN SCOTLAND

The Observer Guide to
Resorts and Hotels

HODDER AND STOUGHTON

PRINTED IN GREAT BRITAIN FOR HODDER
AND STOUGHTON LIMITED, ST. PAUL'S HOUSE,
WARWICK LANE, LONDON, E.C.4 BY C. TINLING
AND CO. LIMITED, LIVERPOOL, LONDON AND
PRESCOT

FOREWORD

"Where to stay and where to eat so that you will get good value for your money" is how a *Financial Times* reviewer summed up the purpose of this series when the first volumes appeared a year ago, greeting it as "a welcome and genuinely new kind of guide".

This is still the briefing with which *The Observer*'s travel writers visit the towns and country places at home and the sunny beaches and ski-slopes abroad that beckon British holiday-makers, making full notes on hotels and restaurants, which are then cross-checked, confirmed and collated by *The Observer*'s "Time Off" staff in London.

No guide-books such as these can be completely comprehensive, and here this applies particularly to some of the islands; nor does the omission of a hotel or restaurant necessarily imply criticism. But inclusion *does* mean that an experienced traveller has found a place worth recommending, as he might recommend it to a friend at home planning his holiday.

Indeed, we should like these books to be thought of as advice from the friend who has just been there himself.

CYRIL RAY,
General Editor

NOTE

Although every effort has been made to ensure the accuracy of the information given in this book, *The Observer* cannot be held responsible for any errors or omissions, or for changes in prices and conditions which may arise. Readers are advised to check when booking.

In this guide, hotel prices quoted by the day or the week are for full board unless otherwise stated.

Appropriate railway stations for places described in this book are given in the text. The future of a number of railway lines in Scotland is uncertain, however, and it is advisable to confirm before a visit that rail services indicated are actually in operation.

CONTENTS

The maps are by Richard Leadbetter

INTRODUCTION

One goes abroad to find unfamiliarity within the bounds of comfort. Scotland is abroad, the closest abroad the English and Welsh have, and in some ways very unfamiliar indeed. Comfort, on the other hand, is spare in Scotland, and this is a consequence of Scotland's not being abroad in the political sense. Despite the efforts of the Scottish Tourist Board, what one may call tourist installations in Scotland often date from the high time of private enterprise; a modern State needs a bit of Government planning and hotel subsidising and corniche-building to keep its attractions in fashion. Poor Scotland has no separate Government.

To Continentals, Scotland is still the country of romantic goings-on: pepper-pot towers and crow-stepped castles and ballads expressing archetypal myths. This suggests that the visitors' Scottish studies have finished at Walter Scott, but there is something true underneath it. For it is a romantic idea that a spectacularly beautiful and wild land should harbour, by the nature of things, giants of the mind. From the weird western lights, the crouching animal shapes of the Scottish landscape, came Burns, Adam Smith, James Hogg and David Hume, whose truth frightened philosophers so much they talked gibberish for a hundred years. Many Scottish ideas are perturbing.

There are a number of different reasons why you may want to go to Scotland. What I enjoy is listening to people's powerful convictions and fantasies against a background of unreasoning hills and seas. In Edinburgh, the shadow of the castle rock falls almost into the multitude of pubs along Rose Street, each patronised by a different set of talkers. Whiskies malt and blended ought to be drunk in a state of some mental excitement; anger or lust will not do, and despair is fatal. So talkers must be found to astound and provoke, and here Scotland can provide.

The best time to go to Scotland is, I think, in late May or in June. The second half of September is often clear, with vast winds

and equinoctial tides that crawl up the shore and over the grass
to where the car stands parked. Avoid July and August if you
can. They are the monsoon months; the rain gets worse towards
early September, and when it clears up in these months midges
swarm out of the steaming bracken: one can get rid of them by
such extremes as lighting a fire of dry cow-pats, but it is ridiculous
to have to walk around in the British Isles with insect repellent
all over you. July, August and early September, the season when
most visitors come to Scotland, have won the country a bad
reputation for weather and comfort.

But in June there is often a heat-wave. On the Atlantic coast
of Argyll, with a slight breeze always moving on the sea, I have
been as hot in June as in Malta in August, without the feeling of
suffocation and searing one gets from the Mediterranean sun.
For some reason, visitors seem to go browner faster in a Highland
June than in southern Europe. The hotels are not yet full, there
are relatively few other visitors on the road, and the bracken is
still green on the hills.

The autumn is often fine: by then the hills are turning russet
as the bracken dies, and the huge currants of west coast gardens
are ready to be picked. And there is another pleasant season,
little known, around Christmas and the New Year, when northern
Scotland sometimes enjoys a few weeks of brilliant calm. The sun
is hot, the air cold as ice (these things can co-exist), and the
hills have a dusting of silver snow. This is also the time when
Scottish people celebrate and draw the stranger into their lives.

One sort of visit, to my mind perfectly satisfying, is to go to
Edinburgh and never move beyond the Pentland Hills to the
south and the river to the north. For some reason, it has been
for years the convention to say how dim and disappointing the
Festival is and a decade of critics have shed crocodile tears over
its "decline". This is tripe. The Festival weeks offer still—in-
creasingly—the most interesting and rewarding, and the wildest,
time in Europe.

Then there are the Highlands. The roads are narrow, but better
than they were, and every year there are more places to stay along
the favourite Inveraray–Oban–Fort William–Skye routes. It
would be idle to describe the beauty of the Highlands, but worth

remembering that this beauty—the silence, the bracken—is the memorial of an immense and inexpiable crime, the expulsion of the Gaelic population by its landlords during the nineteenth century.

Caithness, the green tip of Scotland, is cut off by high moors and extinct volcanoes. Nobody would think of looking for you there, yet there is plenty to see, and the pure glass from the Caithness Glassworks in Wick is to be treasured. The hardy north-east, Buchan and the Mearns, preserves best the Scottish speech and the ballads. Galloway, which involves a left turn after crossing the Border, is an ancient land too often missed by those who feel they can't really have got to Scotland yet.

There is truth in the saying that nobody knows anything about whisky who has not studied it in Scotland. Edinburgh's Rose Street will serve here, but few have ever managed to make their way from one end to the other, taking a sample from each bar. And there is vodka now, as well as whisky—a relief to the younger Scots generation, which finds whisky chasers to its beer too expensive. ("Heavy" is the Scottish for bitter, by the way, and "Export" the most refreshing bottled beer.)

Scottish food is something special, too. Meat is cut in the French manner, and the quality is usually well above that of England, especially beef. "Sausage" in Scotland is a large-calibre thing the size of a mortadella and lightly spiced; one has slices of it fried for breakfast, with the fresh, tender morning rolls that Scottish families insist upon. The well-known dishes, salmon, venison and game birds, are much easier to find than they were a few years ago, and the Aperitif in Edinburgh remains one of the best fish restaurants in the British Isles. Bread is harder and saltier; because of distribution problems the Scots tend to keep their loaves far too long, so that a loaf bought on Friday in Ullapool may very well be a loaf which nobody bought in Paisley on Wednesday. If you cannot stand this prospect, it is better to eat malt and currant loaves or oatcakes, especially oatcakes spread with black treacle from the sugar refineries at Greenock.

Scottish hotels are, on the whole, very much better than they were. The trouble has been that they tried to fulfil a double function: that of bar and gossip exchange for the local community,

11

and that of "high-class hotel" for a dimly-imagined but somehow Edwardian clientele from the south. This used to lead to a frigid, hushed sort of atmosphere, which really covered up a great effort to behave in the respectable manner which the manageress imagined was required of the place. Now things are much less tense, and one can easily enter the "other life" of a small hotel and find uninhibited talk and laughter and anecdote. Everywhere, new bars are being built, grafted oddly on to dark brown walls and under baronial wooden staircases, which allow guests and inhabitants to meet.

A Scottish hotel can always be relied upon to produce a good picnic, too. Indeed, the trouble is sometimes that one is given too much, and the packets of "pancakes" (drop scones in England), jam and cheese scones and cakes makes the meal more like a hungry child's tea than a grown-up's lunch.

What can one do in Scotland? There is, to take an obvious point, much from the past to look at; but two suggestions to add to the conventional lists are Robert Owen's mill settlement on the Falls of Clyde at New Lanark, fountain of one of the main streams in British Socialism, and the haunting series of prehistoric fortresses, carvings, tombs and monuments on the Crinan plain in Argyll, the richest area of Bronze-Age Scotland. Both these sites, I think, are worth many splendid castles in ruins.

One can simply drive and look. One can still, in the old manner, rent a rod on a river or try the trout lochs of a fishing hotel or arrange to go shooting birds or beasts. More satisfying, perhaps, for a family is the west coast practice of "cuddy" fishing, hiring several small boats with fixed-line rods and flies and sailing out to the small reefs and islets where, on summer evenings, the young saithe and lythe rise in frenzied thousands to the surface, snapping at anything that moves. One good night, with six people whisking rods in and out of the water, can produce several hundred fish up to half a pound, and many of them will probably be mackerel. Roasted in buttered paper, they are very good indeed. There is no expertise about cuddy fishing except advice on the night and the place to choose, which most local men can give. Most hotels are on water of some sort, and will provide a dinghy for a family expedition.

It is a mistake to wear fierily-coloured holiday clothes in Scotland. One reason is that most bright clothes are thin. Another is that it puts a visitor at a disadvantage to be visible a long way off. By the time you have arrived, in your sunburst T-shirt, people have had time to prepare an enigmatic smile and to rehearse some perfectly polite remark which will make the bystanders grin for no apparent reason.

Rather for the same reason, it is bad tactics to talk too loudly in Scotland, but this should not be taken to mean that a visitor should whisper empty compliments about the scenery. Scottish conversation, though quiet, is essentially combative; a remark that an Englishman finds frightening is only an invitation to prove his quality by sparring back. The vein is flexible, and in the mouth of a Highlander the words "My goodness, is that really so?" can sound as dangerous as a question from Galileo.

Scotland, in a special way, is easy not to see. To drive over it, enjoy its food and hills and its sea, to visit its monuments, leaves the national reality still secret. A frightful excrescence of tartan boastfulness hides the lack of any political centre to represent the nation and tell it how to speak of its own traditions and secret feelings. The visitor to this beautiful, elusive land is left to make his own judgment upon it: there is no ready-made "Ecosse éternelle" to buy at a counter and take home.

NEAL ASCHERSON

EDINBURGH AND DISTRICT

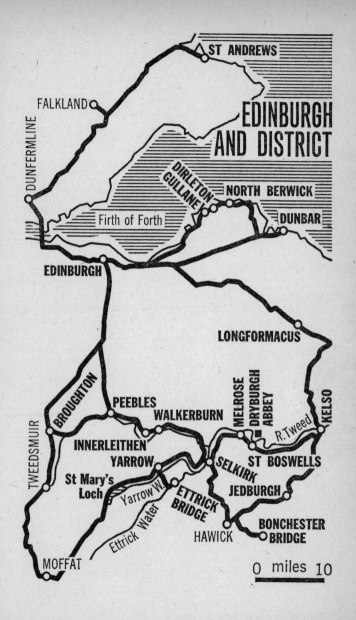

EDINBURGH
AND DISTRICT

0 miles 10

Edinburgh

The capital of Scotland and a city of character and classic beauty, EDINBURGH has a striking setting, dominated by the ancient castle on its crag. The chasm below is laid out with gardens (the railway running through it is comparatively unobtrusive) and beyond is the length of Princes Street, its north side lined with large shops and hotels, the familiar Scott Monument at its eastern end. On the hillside behind Princes Street is the eighteenth-century elegance of the New Town, its spacious streets and squares now the business centre of the city.

The picturesque Old Town is on the castle ridge, descending by way of Castle Hill, Lawnmarket, High Street and Canongate—the Royal Mile—to the Palace of Holyroodhouse, with its memories of Mary Queen of Scots and other Scottish monarchs, and still the royal residence.

Each year for three weeks during late August and early September the Edinburgh International Festival brings added culture and a cosmopolitan air to the city, with artistic events of all kinds attended by visitors of many nationalities.

Visitors to Scotland should set aside a few days to explore Edinburgh, for it has much appeal and the Scots are justly proud of their capital. An added attraction is the nearness of some of the lovely Lowlands coast and country.

London, *373 miles*; Glasgow, *44 miles*; Perth, *62 miles*; Inverness, *176 miles*; Fort William, *146 miles*; Ullapool, *237 miles*.

Rail. Buses. Air services.

Hotels

CALEDONIAN HOTEL, Princes Street (Caledonian 2433). One of the foremost hotels in the city, at the western end of Princes Street. All modern amenities. Of the restaurants in the hotel, Le Postillon is particularly good for cold meals. Set meals from 17s. 6d.; or à la carte. 174 rooms, all with hot and cold water. Many with bath. Bed and breakfast, from 70s. Plus 10 per cent service.

NORTH BRITISH HOTEL, Princes Street (Waverley 2414). A similar large, leading hotel at the Waverley Station end of Princes Street. Meals from 15s. 6d.; or à la carte. 202 rooms, all with hot and cold water, many with bath. Bed and breakfast from 54s. Plus 10 per cent service.

ROYAL BRITISH HOTEL, 20 Princes Street (Waverley 4901). Every comfort. Well situated in Princes Street. Meals from 9s. 6d.; or à la carte. 56 rooms, all with hot and cold water. Bed and breakfast, from 45s. Plus 10 per cent service.

PALACE HOTEL, 1 Castle Street (Caledonian 6222). Another comfortable good-class hotel. In the centre of things on a corner of Princes Street. 42 rooms, all with hot and cold water. Bed and breakfast, 30s.–45s.

GEORGE HOTEL, 19 George Street (Caledonian 1251). High-class hotel of charm and distinction, in the eighteenth-century part of the town just behind Princes Street. Elegant restaurant with dance floor, meals, à la carte. Lounges, bars, hairdressing salon, garage. 90 rooms, all with hot and cold water, many with bath. Bed and breakfast, from 55s. Plus 10 per cent service.

CARLTON HOTEL, North Bridge (Waverley 7277). Conventional, efficiently-run hotel in the city centre, close to Waverley Station and the Royal Mile. Lift, lounge, bar, TV, ballroom, parking and garage near by. Meals, from 11s.; or à la carte. 88 rooms, all with bath and central heating. Bed and breakfast 35s.–50s.

ROYAL STUART HOTEL, Abercromby Place (Waverley 1871). Modern hotel standing in a crescent of the New Town behind Princes Street, overlooking public gardens. Lift, central heating, garage and parking space near by. 64 rooms, all with hot and cold water and fires, a few with bath. Bed and breakfast 35s.–40s. Day, 48s.–54s. Plus 10 per cent service.

ROXBURGHE HOTEL, Charlotte Square (Caledonian 6254). Well-established hotel just off Princes Street, on one of the oldest and most graceful of the Georgian squares, overlooking gardens. It is a charming building and the interior furnishing includes antiques and some fine prints. 66 rooms, all with hot and cold water, many with bath. Bed and breakfast, 52s. 6d.–80s. Week, from 20 gn. Plus 10 per cent service.

ADAM HOTEL, 19 Lansdowne Crescent, Edinburgh 12 (Donaldson 1148). Congenial small hotel in a quiet crescent in the West End district, within a few minutes of Princes Street. Good food; dinner, 10s. 6d. (no lunch). Unlicensed. 12 rooms, all with hot and cold water. Bed and breakfast, 30s.–35s.

BRAID HILLS HOTEL, Braid Road, Edinburgh 10 (Morningside 6291). Comfortable hotel quietly placed in its own grounds on the city outskirts, with a view over Edinburgh. A good choice for those with a car. Lounges, bars, central heating. 49 rooms, all with hot and cold water. Bed and breakfast, 37s. 6d.–45s. Week, 19–21 gn.

DONMAREE HOTEL, Mayfield Gardens, Edinburgh 9 (New 3641). Beyond the Old Town, on the main road south. On bus routes to the city centre, but best suited to motorists. Well kept, with garden, bar, TV; garage. 25 rooms, all with hot and cold water and electric fire or central heating. Bed and breakfast, 30s.–45s. Week, 17–21 gn. Plus 10 per cent service.

THE HAWES INN, South Queensferry (South Queensferry 215). In attractive surroundings on the Firth of Forth nine or ten miles out of Edinburgh, where the little town of South Queensferry has grown up round the estuary crossing. The inn faces the little old ferry, with the massive Forth railway bridge on one side and the more elegant new road bridge on the other. Historic in origin, the interior has been tastefully modernised. Particularly recommended for a meal and excursion outside the city. The restaurant is charming but has about six tables only, so booking is advisable. Food and service excellent; interesting but by no means cheap à la carte menu. Lounges and bars. Open all the year. 10 rooms, with hot and cold water. Bed and breakfast, 35s.–42s.

Restaurants

CAFÉ ROYAL, 17 West Register Street (Waverley 1884). In a narrow street off the eastern end of Princes Street (behind Woolworths), this is one of Edinburgh's leading restaurants. Calm, comfortable and unostentatious; the name gives a clue to the Edwardian décor and atmosphere. The Oyster Bar on the ground floor is a good choice for lunch, and so is the agreeable Crown Room upstairs; both have a four-course set meal at around 9s. 6d., or à la carte. The more formal Barbecue Grill is the main restaurant and has the most elaborate menu. Plenty of fish. Cooking and presentation are well done; the service is pleasing. Allow at least 30s. for a good meal. Advisable to book. Closed Sundays.

THE APERITIF, 24 Frederick Street (Caledonian 6066). Smart, expensive restaurant just off Princes Street. Particularly noted for its fish, but dishes of all kinds on the wide à la carte menu. Efficient service. Advisable to book. Closed Sundays.

HANDSEL RESTAURANT, 22 Stafford Street (Caledonian 5522). An excellent place, with a snappy Continental air unusual in Scotland. In an attractive Georgian house behind the west end of Princes Street; Regency-style interior. The food is interesting and appetising; good à la carte choice. Service quick and courteous. Allow around 30s. for an unstinted but not extravagant meal. The separate Blue Room has a Scandinavian cold table; ground-floor bar. Advisable to book. Closed Sundays.

DORIC TAVERN, 15 Market Street (Caledonian 1084). Busy, informal small restaurant, below North Bridge by Waverley Station. The first-floor room has about a dozen tables, with adjoining bar. Friendly atmosphere; food nicely cooked and served. Three-course lunch, 6s. 6d.; four-course dinner, 9s.; main dishes, à la carte, 5s. 6d.–10s. 6d.

DENMARK ROOM, The Albyn, 77 Queen Street. Down the area steps below the less exciting Albyn Restaurant. Plain room in functional modern style, where light meals are served speedily and informally. The menu consists of excellent soups, good open sandwiches and salads, cheese and coffee; lager or cider from the bar make a good accompaniment. Satisfying lunch for about 6s. or 7s.

LAIGH COFFEE HOUSE, 83 Hanover Street (Caledonian 1552). Self-service basement coffee bar in the bright, contemporary manner.

Imaginative salads and sandwiches for quick, cheap snacks; coffee reasonably good. Varied clientele, with the emphasis on youth. Off Princes Street, and convenient for a pause while shopping or sightseeing. Closed Sundays.

CRAMOND INN, Cramond (Davidsons Mains 2035). Outside Edinburgh, on the Firth of Forth a few miles downstream from the bridges, this is an old, whitewashed inn, in the little fishing village of Cramond. Well known for its good food and much frequented by local people. Agreeably informal and not too expensive. Advisable to book. Closed Sundays.

St Andrews

Immediately north of Edinburgh, the small and fertile county of Fife occupies the peninsula between the Firth of Forth and Firth of Tay.

On its seaward coast is the historic university city of ST ANDREWS. The university, founded in 1412, is the oldest in Scotland, and the city was also for many years the ecclesiastical centre of the country, having connections with John Knox. The colleges, the churches and the houses are all delightfully redolent of the past, and you can wander for hours along the streets of the town.

There are four golf courses at St Andrews, and everything possible is done for the golfer. There are also good sands, and southwards, in the district curiously known as the East Neuk, there are a string of lost little fishing ports to be explored—Crail, Anstruther, Pittenweem, Elie—some of the houses still with the old step-gables.

Inland, the picturesque little town of Falkland is worth a visit for sixteenth-century Falkland Palace, and at Dunfermline the fine abbey church contains the grave of Robert the Bruce. Culross, on the shore of the Firth of Forth, is a living example of a Scottish town of the sixteenth and seventeenth centuries.

St Andrews–Edinburgh, *49 miles*; Dundee, *11 miles* (using ferry);
Perth, *31 miles.*
Rail. Buses.
County: Fife.

Hotels

SCORES HOTEL (St Andrews 82). Comfortable hotel of a high
standard, facing the sea and near the golf courses. 40 rooms, all
with hot and cold water, a few with bath. Bed and breakfast,
35s.–37s. 6d. Day, 40s.–60s.

STAR HOTEL, Market Street (St Andrews 698). De-luxe business-
man's hotel in the town centre. Lounges, bar. Open all the year.
23 rooms, all with hot and cold water, some with bath. Bed and
breakfast, 30s.–42s. Week, 13–18 gn. Plus 5 per cent service.

KINBURN HOTEL, Double Dykes Road (St Andrews 620). Un-
assuming hotel, particularly popular among golfers. Unlicensed.
No dogs. Open all the year. 24 rooms, all with hot and cold water.
Bed and breakfast, 27s. 6d.–30s. Week, 12–15 gn.

RUFFLETS HOTEL (St Andrews 249). Modern country-house hotel
about two miles outside St Andrews. It would suit those with a
car seeking rural peace close to the charming town. Every comfort,
including three lounges, bar, gardens with putting green, central
heating. Pretty cottage annexe. No dogs. Open March–December. 20 rooms, all with hot and cold water, some with bath. Bed
and breakfast, 30s.–40s. Week, 14½–18 gn.

East Lothian Coast

The East Lothian coast, just to the east of Edinburgh, has a
number of resorts which offer a variety of holiday facilities and
are particularly known for their rocks, cliffs and sandy bays, for
their golf, and their record of dry, sunny weather.

GULLANE is a small centre on the Firth of Forth. Just beyond
and a little inland is the delightful village of DIRLETON. A few
miles farther is NORTH BERWICK, a leading East Lothian resort,

and, on the North Sea coast, DUNBAR, an old fishing port between cliffs.

Edinburgh–North Berwick, *24 miles*; North Berwick–Dunbar, *13 miles*; Edinburgh–Gullane, *19 miles*.

Railway stations: North Berwick, Dunbar. Buses.

County: East Lothian.

Hotels   Gullane

GREYWALLS HOTEL (Gullane 2144). A large country house in a pleasant walled garden, with views of the Firth of Forth and across the golf course. Open Easter to mid-October. 20 rooms, with hot and cold water, some with bath. Bed and breakfast, from 40s. Week, 17–20 gn.

Dirleton

THE OPEN ARMS (Dirleton 241). Best known as an eating house with a varied menu and wine list. Meals, à la carte. Log fires in the lounges; well-kept garden. Open all the year (closed Mondays November–March). Three rooms. Bed and breakfast, 42s. 6d.–47s. 6d.

North Berwick

MARINE HOTEL (North Berwick 2406). Agreeable, rather grand hotel, nicely set in a garden looking across the links to the sea. Lift; lounges, billiards, dancing, garage. Two hard tennis courts, putting green, golf practice in grounds. 86 rooms, all with hot and cold water. Bed and breakfast, 37s. 6d.–50s. Week, 17–26 gn.

ROYAL HOTEL (North Berwick 2401). Near the station and not far from the beach. Garden, lounge, TV, garage. 43 rooms, all with hot and cold water, a few with bath. Bed and breakfast, 32s. 6d.–40s. Week, 17–20 gn.

WESTERDUNES HOTEL (North Berwick 520). Country-house hotel in 17 acres of grounds. About 200 yards from the sea, a right-of-way across the golf course giving access to a fine beach; small swimming-pool and tennis court in the grounds, squash court. Table d'hote and à la carte meals. Open May–September. 30 rooms, all with hot and cold water, a few with bath. Bed and breakfast, from 30s.

Dunbar

ROXBURGHE MARINE HOTEL (Dunbar 2155). Well-kept hotel in its own grounds, near the golf course and overlooking the sea. Comfort and atmosphere suited to families. Lounges, central heating. Open all the year. 48 rooms, all with hot and cold water. Bed and breakfast, from 25s. Week, 13–17 gn.

The Border Country

So easily reached from England or from Edinburgh, yet too often missed by visitors eager to get to the Highlands, the Border Country is a grand and lovely district of rich green valleys, rolling moorland hills and the River Tweed.

It is now a prosperous agricultural region, mainly concerned with sheep farming and the woollen industry, yet history, romance and literature mingle in an atmosphere thick with memories of the fierce struggles against the English, of the great abbeys now in ruins, and of Sir Walter Scott and his contemporaries.

Leisurely exploring is a pleasure in such peace and space; gentle or strenuous walks abound; and there is excellent salmon and trout fishing.

Peebles and District

Only a short distance immediately south of Edinburgh, PEEBLES makes a good starting point for exploration of the Borders and has become a holiday centre for the district. An endearing little grey town, it stands on the banks of the Tweed in a lush, wooded valley beneath gently rounded hills.

A few miles eastwards along the Tweed are INNERLEITHEN and WALKERBURN, unremarkable woollen mill villages but well placed for sightseeing, country walks and fishing. Traquair House, across the Tweed from Innerleithen, is worth a visit as "the oldest inhabited house in Scotland" (open daily, June–September; Sundays only, April and May).

Edinburgh–Peebles, *25 miles*; Peebles–Innerleithen, *6 miles*; Peebles–Melrose, *22 miles*.

Railway stations: Edinburgh, Galashiels. Buses.

County: Peeblesshire.

Hotels   Peebles

TONTINE HOTEL (Peebles 3392). An old coaching inn in the High Street, modernised with taste and comfort; agreeable lounge and dining-room. The new wing at the back has excellent rooms of contemporary design, some overlooking the river and hills. Service good; food reasonably so. Garage and parking space. Open all the year. 14 rooms with hot and cold water in main building; 16 rooms, all with bath, in new wing. Bed and breakfast, 32s. 6d.–47s. 6d. Day, 54s.–63s. Plus 10 per cent service.

PEEBLES HYDRO (Peebles 3102). For those wanting a spacious, rather grand hotel with every comfort and facility, including lounges, bar, TV, ballroom, tennis, badminton, indoor swimming-pool, lift, central heating. In its own grounds on the hillside above the town, looking across the valley. Open all the year. 170 rooms, all with hot and cold water, some with bath. Day, 49s.–81s. 6d. Plus 10 per cent service.

VENLAW CASTLE HOTEL (Peebles 2384). Country house peacefully set among fields and woods in the hills outside the town, reached by a rather rough track from the Edinburgh road. Unassuming and homely; rooms rather bare but provided with essentials. Open all the year. 14 rooms, with hot and cold water. Bed and breakfast, 27s. 6d.–30s. Week, 12½–13½ gn.

Innerleithen

TIGHNUILT HOTEL (Innerleithen 233). Stands on its own in the country, outside the village on the way to Peebles. In a garden just above the road, with peaceful views of valley, river and hills.

Comfort and atmosphere of a private house, with a cosy lounge and spacious, cheerful bedrooms. Friendly owners. No lunch, but picnic meals on request. Dinner, 12s. 6d. Open Easter–end September. 6 rooms, with hot and cold water. Bed and breakfast, 25s.–30s.

Walkerburn

TWEED VALLEY HOTEL (Walkerburn 220). On the village edge, in a garden above the road, with the Tweed just below and fields all round. Well-kept country-house hotel. Very much a fishing place, with salmon and trout fishing courses in spring and autumn; instruction also available at other times in the season for individuals or small parties; rods and reels for hire. Open all the year. 15 rooms, all with hot and cold water. Bed and breakfast, 25s. Week, 11 gn.

Melrose and Dryburgh

An agreeable small town in the Tweed valley, MELROSE nestles at the foot of the triple-peaked Eildon Hills, which rise sudden and solitary from the rich green countryside, making a distinctive landmark for miles.

The pride of Melrose is its abbey. Although in ruins now, the beauty of the architectural lines, the carvings and the delicate tracery of the windows can be seen to great advantage, outlined bare against the sky. Like the other great Border abbeys, Melrose was founded by King David I in the twelfth century; its history was disturbed by English raids and it was a semi-ruin even before the Reformation came to Scotland.

On the Tweed about three miles west of Melrose lies Abbotsford, last home of Sir Walter Scott, who knew and loved the Border Country all his life, lived there for many years and used it for the setting of many of his stories. The house is open daily from April–October.

From Melrose towards ST BOSWELLS and Dryburgh, the Tweed flows calm and broad through a prosperous, well-ordered land of lush woods and pastures rolling away to a wide panorama of distant hills—the Cheviots, which mark the boundary with England.

Dryburgh Abbey has a glorious setting in a wooded hollow on the banks of the Tweed. Only fragments of the buildings remain, but it is the most romantic of the abbeys. Sir Walter Scott and Earl Haig are buried here with other members of ancient Border families.

Edinburgh–Melrose, *37 miles*; Melrose–St Boswells, *4 miles*; Melrose–Kelso, *14 miles*.

Railway stations: Melrose, St Boswells. Buses.

County: Roxburghshire.

Hotels   Melrose

GEORGE AND ABBOTSFORD HOTEL (Melrose 308). In the town centre. Conventional but agreeable hotel, efficiently run and prettily furnished. Bar, lounge; restaurant, where the motto is "any meal at any time"; small inner garden. Fishing for guests on a stretch of the Tweed. Open all the year. 30 rooms, all with hot and cold water, a few with bath. Bed and breakfast, from 39s. 6d. Day, 63s. 6d.

BURT'S HOTEL (Melrose 85). On the central square, a simple family hotel with a friendly welcome. For those seeking plain accommodation at a reasonable price. Lounge, bar, small garden. Open all the year. 17 rooms, with hot and cold water. Bed and breakfast, 28s.–30s. Week, 11–12 gn.

St Boswells

DRYBURGH ABBEY HOTEL (St Boswells 2261). Beautifully placed in restful surroundings beside the ruins. Traditional country-house hotel in the Scottish baronial manner; spacious halls and lounges; extensive grounds. Hushed, genteel atmosphere most suited to the elderly; a car is essential as the situation is remote. Open May–October. 32 rooms, all with hot and cold water. Bed and breakfast, 35s. Week, 15 gn.

Kelso

Set among meadows and parkland beside the peaceful Tweed, KELSO has an air of elegance and well-being. The sleepy streets of the little town converge on the charming eighteenth-century square; the abbey ruins dominate the scene. The pleasures here are pastoral—fishing and walks, and perhaps a race meeting or other local event enjoyed by the farming community.
Edinburgh, *43 miles*; Peebles, *35 miles*; Jedburgh, *12 miles*.
Rail. Buses.
County: Roxburghshire.

Hotel

EDNAM HOUSE HOTEL (Kelso 68). Rambling, old-fashioned country house backing on the river; views across the water meadows from the garden and roof-terrace, the restaurant and many of the rooms. Family run, with a pleasing, not too formal atmosphere. Attractive, up-to-date accommodation in the two modern wings. Many guests come for the fishing; there is a salmon and trout beat immediately in front of the hotel and other fishing can be arranged near by. Open all the year. 40 rooms, all with hot and cold water, some with bath. Bed and breakfast, from 32s. 6d. Week, 15–21 gn.

Longformacus

As you travel eastwards from Kelso into Berwickshire, the country becomes flatter and less interesting. Passing through the agricultural villages of Coldstream, Greenlaw and Duns, you can climb into the lonely Lammermuir Hills, where moorland rolls away for miles around you, the only sign of life an occasional cottage for the shepherds tending the wandering sheep.

Undisturbed in the midst of these bleak moors is the remote hamlet of LONGFORMACUS. An engaging group of a handful of stone cottages and a general store, it shelters in the tree-filled valley of the Whiteadder Water.

Edinburgh, *32 miles*; Kelso, *23 miles*; Duns, *7 miles*.
County: Berwickshire.

Hotel

RATHBURNE HOTEL (Longformacus 232). By the stream half-a-mile up the valley, this former shooting lodge is now a hotel of character, ideal for those who like to stay out in the wilds yet in a civilised atmosphere. The enterprising young owners have arranged the house with style; bright décor in lounges and bar, cheered by log fires; plain bedrooms. Unassuming comfort and friendly informality are the keynote; families welcome. Country people gather in the public bar at the back, the only "local" for miles. Trout fishing in surrounding waters; fishing courses held from time to time. The Borders, Edinburgh and the coast easily reached by car; petrol pump at hotel. Open all the year. 12 rooms, all with hot and cold water. Bed and breakfast, 27s. 6d. Week, 16 gn.

Jedburgh District

In wooded, parklike countryside on the Jed Water, JEDBURGH is one of the quaintest and most characterful of the Border towns. Streets and cobbled alleys lined with mellow stone cottages climb the hill to the abbey. Roofless, but with walls and towers still largely intact, this is a splendid sight.

The border is only a few miles south at Carter Bar, the magnificently wild and empty hills making a fitting boundary between two countries. Shunning England, you can take the upland road which leads back through BONCHESTER BRIDGE to Hawick, an important centre of the knitwear industry.

Jedburgh–Kelso, *12 miles*; Jedburgh–Hawick, *11 miles*; Bonchester Bridge–Hawick, *8 miles*.
Railway station: Hawick. Buses.
County: Roxburghshire.

Hotels   Jedburgh

JED FOREST HOTEL (Camptown 204). Four or five miles from Jedburgh on the way to Carter Bar, this is an attractive stone-built house in a hollow off the main road. Plain but acceptable accommodation. Much used by passing motorists for overnight stops and meals. Lounge, bar. Open all the year. 8 rooms, with hot and cold water. Bed and breakfast, 30s. Week, 15 gn.

Bonchester Bridge

WOLFELEE HOTEL (Bonchester Bridge 202). Take a narrow turning at the top of the hill outside Bonchester Bridge to reach this excellent hotel, standing in its own grounds in wooded country. An old Scottish house complete with gables and turrets, it is impeccably kept and arranged with great charm, modern amenities not spoiling the period flavour. Spacious panelled lounges and halls; the fresh, pretty bedrooms are a delight; upper floors close-carpeted throughout. Absolute peace and isolation. Simple, well-prepared meals, served with care. Helpful staff. Closed in January and February. 13 rooms, all with hot and cold water, some with bath. Bed and breakfast, 32s. 6d. Week, 16 gn. Plus 10 per cent service.

Selkirk and District

Tiered up a hillside above Ettrick Water, grey roofs and spires rising from the trees, SELKIRK has a somewhat Continental aspect from a distance, although briskly Scottish enough in character.

One of the chief Common Riding ceremonies of the Borders takes place here in mid-June. These events survive from the days of unrest when the townspeople rode round their boundaries to maintain ownership. Flodden Field is remembered vividly, too, and the climax of the Selkirk celebrations is the casting of the colours, commemorating the return from the disastrous battle of the lone Selkirk survivor, bearing a captured English flag.

Two of the best-known rivers of the district meet just west of Selkirk, the Ettrick and the Yarrow, famed for their gentle beauty, their fishing and their literary associations. Above the valleys stretch extensive moors, where the hardy can walk in solitude and naturalists find interesting plants and birds.

Melrose, *7 miles*; Jedburgh, *17 miles*; Peebles, *21 miles*.

Buses.

County: Selkirkshire.

Hotels   Selkirk

HEATHERLIE HILL HOTEL (Selkirk 3200). Quietly placed, in a sheltered garden on a hill leading up to the town. Sprucely kept and restful; unelaborate comfort; suited to older people. Lounge with TV, residents' bar. Open Easter–November. 11 rooms, with hot and cold water. Bed and breakfast, from 25s. Week, from 10½ gn.

WOODBURN HOTEL (Selkirk 3372). Next to the Heatherlie Hill, in a similar peaceful position, the garden sloping down to a stream. Easygoing family atmosphere. Pleasant lounge and bar. Open all the year. 4 rooms, with hot and cold water. Bed and breakfast, from 23s. 6d. Week, from 10 gn.

Ettrick Bridge

ETTRICK SHAWS HOTEL (Ettrick Bridge 229). In a rural setting on the banks of Ettrick Water, a mile or two up the valley from Ettrick Bridge. A spacious house; rather bare, but pleasing, with attractive lounge, dining-room and bar. Active, enthusiastic owners; family atmosphere. The accent is on fishing; the hotel has its own half-mile stretch of river for salmon and trout; fishing courses held in the spring. Open all the year. 9 rooms, with hot and cold water. Bed and breakfast, from 25s. Week, 12 gn.

Scotland welcomes you . . .

You'll succumb to the magic of
Scotland . . . the remote glens, the
towering mountains, the incomparable
scenery. Something for everyone ;
ski-ing, boating, fishing, golf ; modern
cities, ancient castles ; fine resorts,
modern hotels, boarding houses,
hostels, camps. No country offers a
greater variety than Scotland.

*For all details about Scotland
write to Room 31*

THE SCOTTISH TOURIST BOARD
2 RUTLAND PLACE, EDINBURGH, I.

Yarrow

GORDON ARMS HOTEL (Yarrow 204). Isolated moorland fishing inn on the Yarrow about 12 miles upstream from Selkirk. In modest country-pub style; nicely kept. Small lounges and bar. Open all the year. 4 rooms. Bed and breakfast, 27s. 6d. Week, 11 gn.

St Mary's Loch

Higher up the Yarrow valley is ST MARY'S LOCH, about three miles long and the largest in southern Scotland. Fishing is popular and there is walking in the hills enclosing the water. The loch is of interest, too, for its connections with Scott and his associates, particularly his poet friend James Hogg, the Ettrick Shepherd, whose statue stands on the shore.

The wild scenery increases in grandeur as the mountains steepen beyond the loch and the road climbs the pass, to descend the further slope between craggy heights and rushing torrents and through a beautiful valley to Moffat. The whole region has an austere beauty, quite different from the softer valley of the Tweed. Selkirk, *18 miles*; Moffat, *16 miles*; Peebles, *20 miles*.

County: Selkirkshire.

Hotels

TIBBIE SHIEL'S INN (Cappercleuch 211). A little whitewashed inn standing among trees by the water at the head of the loch, the smaller Loch of the Lowes just behind. Tibbie Shiel was the first licensee, a forthright local character who gathered about her Scott, Hogg and other literary figures of the nineteenth century. This early fame has lasted and the inn is widely known for its simple rural comfort and the beauty and romance of its surroundings. Trout fishing in the loch free to residents; boats for hire. Lounge, bar. Open all the year. 8 rooms, all with hot and cold water. Bed and breakfast, 27s. 6d. Week, 12½ gn.

RODONO HOTEL (Cappercleuch 212). Fishing hotel in a sunny,

elevated position midway along the loch, with views across the water. Homelike and unassuming. Guests have free trout fishing in the loch, and the seven-mile Meggat Water is exclusively for their use; anglers' drying-room; boats for hire. Two lounges, bar, terrace. Open all the year. 14 rooms, all with hot and cold water. Bed and breakfast, from 25s. Week, 11–12 gn.

Tweedsmuir District

Turning north from Moffat, up into the hills again and past the Devil's Beef Tub, a deep cleft in the land said to have been a hideout of Border cattle rustlers, travellers soon pick up the Tweed at its source and follow it as it winds down to Tweedsmuir through gloriously wild moorland. As the river flows on towards BROUGHTON and PEEBLES, the valley becomes green and smiling, rich farmland and woods on either hand, the moors above.
Moffat, *15 miles*; Peebles, *18 miles*; Edinburgh, *37 miles*.
Buses.
County: Peeblesshire.

Hotel   Broughton

MOSSFENNAN FARM HOTEL, Broughton, by Biggar (Broughton 225). Some miles down the valley from Tweedsmuir village, near the crossroads for Peebles and Broughton, this attractive farmhouse stands off the road in a sheltered garden, surrounded by fields. A charming place, particularly for older people wanting quietness at a price very reasonable for the attention provided. Delightful first-floor lounge with views of the hills; pleasing bedrooms furnished in solid, old-fashioned country style. Unlicensed. Open April–September (shooting parties take much of the accommodation in August and September). 9 rooms, some with hot and cold water; 3 bathrooms. Bed and breakfast, 21s. Week, 9 gn.

THE SOUTH-WEST

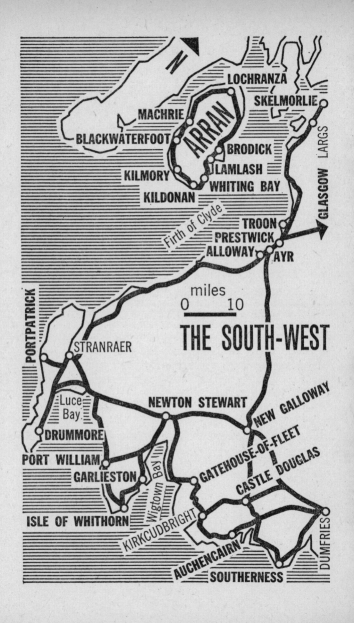

Galloway

Galloway is the name given to the counties of Wigtown and Kirkcudbright in the south-western corner of Scotland. A little-known district, it deserves wider attention, for the countryside of hills, woods, lochs and rivers is wild and beautiful; the attractive rocky coast has sandy bays; and the towns and villages are quiet, agreeable small places ideal as centres for touring and for walking, bathing, fishing and golf.

New Galloway, Castle Douglas and District

Some distance inland, at the northern end of Loch Ken, NEW GALLOWAY is an unspoilt little town that would make an admirable centre from which to explore Galloway. The scenery along Loch Ken is magnificent and there is boating and fishing; also golf and hill walking.

South of New Galloway and four or five miles from the coast, the market town and holiday resort of CASTLE DOUGLAS is also convenient for excursions. It is in pleasant, undulating country of woods and fields, with salmon and trout fishing in rivers and lochs.

On the coast of the Solway Firth near by, the seaside village of AUCHENCAIRN has a lovely setting on a bay, and to the east is the quiet little resort of SOUTHERNESS.

Edinburgh–New Galloway, *86 miles*; New Galloway–Castle Douglas, *14 miles*.

Railway stations: Castle Douglas, New Galloway, Dumfries. Buses.

County: Kirkcudbrightshire.

Hotels   New Galloway

CROSS KEYS HOTEL (New Galloway 218). Unassuming, agreeable hotel in the main street. Open all the year. 9 rooms, all with hot and cold water. Bed and breakfast, from 28s. Week, 13–14 gn.

MILTON PARK HOTEL, Dalry (Dalry 286). Country-house hotel standing in its own grounds in the valley of the Ken, just north of New Galloway. Lounges, TV, tennis and croquet. Good fishing available for guests. Open mid-March to mid-October. 17 rooms, all with hot and cold water. Bed and breakfast, 27s. 6d. Week, 14 gn. Plus 10 per cent service.

Castle Douglas

DOUGLAS ARMS HOTEL (Castle Douglas 2231). Delightful, modernised hotel, once an old coaching inn. In the town centre at a busy crossroads, it might be noisy. Lounges, restaurant, bar. Open all the year. 24 rooms, all with hot and cold water and central heating. Bed and breakfast, from 36s. Week, from 16 gn.

CULGRUFF HOUSE HOTEL, Crossmichael (Crossmichael 230). This comfortable, homely hotel has a good reputation and the advantage of being in a quiet, isolated position in the country several miles north of the town. Lounges; central heating. Open all the year. 17 rooms, with hot and cold water. Week, from 12 gn.

Auchencairn

BALCARY BAY HOTEL (Auchencairn 17). Family hotel in a beautiful, secluded position on the edge of a bay, with safe bathing from the private beach. Children welcome. Fishing, golf near by, good walking. Open all the year. 15 rooms, with hot and cold water. Bed and breakfast, 25s.–35s. Week, 10–15 gn.

Southerness-on-Solway

PAUL JONES HOTEL, Southerness-on-Solway, by Dumfries (Kirkbean 205). Agreeable small hotel in peaceful country close to the shore of the Solway Firth, all rooms overlooking the sea. Lounge with TV, sun parlour. Championship golf course and tennis courts alongside the hotel; fishing, wildfowling in season. Open all the year. 6 rooms, all with hot and cold water. Week, 12 gn.

Wigtown Bay

This large bay lies to the west of CASTLE DOUGLAS. On its eastern side is GATEHOUSE-OF-FLEET, a quiet country town slightly inland on the Water of Fleet. There is a sand beach about three miles away.

A lovely coast road leads up to the head of the bay and to the active little town of NEWTON STEWART, set on the River Cree in beautiful country of hills, woods and moorland. Farther inland and easily explored by car is wild, grandiose Glen Trool with its loch, in the heart of the remote Galloway Highlands, where there is the Glen Trool National Forest Park. Here Robert Bruce beat the English troops.

On the western shore of Wigtown Bay, GARLIESTON is a small place of a certain charm; beyond, ISLE OF WHITHORN is an attractive little port (which in spite of its name is on the mainland), at the mouth of the bay. Both villages are completely quiet, and untroubled by modern holiday developments.

Throughout the district there is excellent river and loch fishing, as well as golf, shooting, walking, bathing and boating.

Castle-Douglas – Gatehouse-of-Fleet, *15 miles*; Gatehouse-of-Fleet–Newton Stewart, *19 miles*; Newton Stewart–Whithorn, *18 miles*; Newton Stewart–Stranraer, *25 miles*.

Railway stations: Gatehouse-of-Fleet, Newton Stewart. Buses. Counties: Kirkcudbrightshire (Gatehouse-of-Fleet); Wigtownshire (Newton Stewart, Garlieston, Whithorn).

Hotels   Gatehouse-of-Fleet

MURRAY ORMS (Gatehouse 207). Pleasant hotel in the town, long established as the local inn. Most comfortable, with well-cooked meals. Lounges, bar, games room. Open all the year. 10 rooms in the hotel and 10 in the annexes, all with hot and cold water. Bed and breakfast, from 28s. 6d. Week, 12–17 gn. Plus 10 per cent service.

CALLY HOTEL (Gatehouse 341). Large eighteenth-century mansion in extensive park and gardens. A comfortable hotel, ideal for those who want complete peace and quiet, particularly older people. Lounges, TV lounges, bar, billiards, table tennis, hair-dressing salon. Hard tennis court, croquet, putting and children's playground in the park; also lake for boating and fishing; sandy beaches near by. Special children's high tea. Open Easter to mid-October. 79 rooms, all with hot and cold water, some with bath. Bed and breakfast, 35s.–50s. Week, 17–23 gn.

Newton Stewart

CREEBRIDGE HOUSE HOTEL (Newton Stewart 372). This pretty house in a lovely garden makes a charming and comfortable hotel and a good base from which to explore Galloway. Close to the town centre and to the river, where there is fishing. Lounges, bar. Open all the year. 15 rooms, all with hot and cold water. Bed and breakfast, 25s.–27s. 6d. Week, 11–12 gn.

KIRROUGHTREE HOUSE HOTEL (Newton Stewart 141). A hotel of a high standard a mile or so east of the town, on the edge of the golf course. The service is friendly and the meals good. Open all the year. 14 rooms, most with hot and cold water. Bed and breakfast, 28s. Week, 14 gn.

Garlieston

QUEEN'S ARMS HOTEL (Garlieston 233). Modest hotel suitable for a simple family holiday. Pleasant owners. 5 rooms, with hot and cold water. Bed and breakfast, from 18s. Week, 10–14 gn.

Isle of Whithorn

STEAM PACKET HOTEL (Whithorn 334). This little inn down by the harbour has been modernised, with attractively decorated bedrooms. The owner tries to provide interesting food, including local lobster. Lounge, bar. Shooting, fishing and boating can be arranged. Open March–September. 4 rooms, all with bath. Bed and breakfast, 27s. 6d.–30s. Week, 16 gn.

CASTLEWIGG FARM HOTEL, Whithorn (Whithorn 213). A modest hotel that welcomes children. About two miles from Whithorn on the road to Newton Stewart, and five miles from the sea; bathing, golf, fishing are within reach. Lounge with TV, bar, central heating. 9 rooms, all with hot and cold water. Week, 11 gn.

Luce Bay

Wide, open Luce Bay has reddish sand beaches and strange, jutting rocks along its shores, with wild country behind. Remote little seaside villages provide modest accommodation for those with a car seeking peace and unorganised bathing, boating and fishing.

PORT WILLIAM has a lovely situation on the eastern shore and fine views across the bay to DRUMMORE. From there it is worth continuing the few miles to the Mull of Galloway, the most southerly point on the mainland of Scotland, where dramatic rocks fall sheer to the sea. PORTPATRICK on the west coast of the Rhinns of Galloway Peninsula, is a popular resort and fishing harbour, with sandy bays for bathing, salmon and trout fishing and two golf courses.

Newton Stewart–Port William, *17 miles*; Newton Stewart–Drummore, *34 miles*; Portpatrick–Stranraer, *8 miles*.

Railway stations: Stranraer, Newton Stewart. Buses.

County: Wigtownshire.

Hotels   Port William

MONREITH ARMS HOTEL (Port William 232). Simple but congenial, reasonably comfortable small hotel. Helpful owners. Lounge, bar. Open all the year. 18 rooms, all with hot and cold water. Bed and breakfast, 27s. 6d.–30s. Week, 11–14 gn.

Drummore

THE QUEEN'S HOTEL (Drummore 331). Modest little hotel overlooking the bay and close to the beach. Local fish and farm produce. Lounges, bar; fitted carpets. Open all the year. 11 rooms, most with hot and cold water. Week, 11½ gn.

Portpatrick

ROSLIN HOTEL (Portpatrick 241). This well-run hotel is on the hill a few minutes from the harbour and next to the golf course; views of the sea. Open Easter to end-September. 13 rooms, all with hot and cold water. Bed and breakfast, 23s. 6d. Week, 11 gn.

PORTPATRICK HOTEL (Portpatrick 333). Large, comfortable establishment on the cliffs above the harbour. Lounges, bar, games room. Open May–end September. 58 rooms, all with hot and cold water, some with bath. Bed and breakfast, from 35s. Week, 12–23 gn. Plus 10 per cent service.

Ayrshire Coast

Stretching northwards from Galloway, the Ayrshire coast has a series of resorts, their sandy beaches and proximity to Glasgow and other industrial centres making them popular for a conventional seaside holiday. Entertainments for visitors are many, with the emphasis on bathing, boating and golf.

The sea port and county town of AYR faces across the Firth of Clyde to the Isle of Arran and is famous for its Burns association. The sandy beach is more than two miles long, and there are two golf courses. Clyde steamers cruise to the mainland and islands. Near-by ALLOWAY is full of memories of Burns, with a museum and the cottage where he was born.

An important industrial town close to Ayr, PRESTWICK offers a wide, sandy beach, a large swimming-pool and several golf courses. TROON, a few miles beyond, is a well-known port and golfing resort. It is set on a narrow spit of land between Ayr Bay and Irvine Bay, and sandy beaches and headlands extend on either side; there are several excellent golf courses. The town has gracious parks and private houses.

On Wemyss Bay on the northern boundary of Ayrshire, SKELMORLIE has a fine beach and views across the Firth of Clyde to Bute. There are boat trips, and there is a measured mile opposite the resort where small boats are speed-tested.

Edinburgh-Ayr, *72 miles*; Castle Douglas–Ayr, *51 miles*; Ayr–Skelmorlie, *30 miles*.

Railway stations: Ayr, Prestwick, Troon, Wemyss Bay. Airport: Prestwick. Buses. Steamers.

Hotels   Ayr

STATION HOTEL (Ayr 63268/9). Modernised, comfortable hotel in the town centre five minutes from the sea. The food is well cooked and presented. Open all the year. 75 rooms, all with hot and cold water, some with bath. Bed and breakfast, from 40s. Day, 57s. 6d.

MARINE COURT HOTEL (Ayr 65261). About 200 yards from the beach, this is a really charming hotel with a garden and pretty views over the fields. It stands in a cul-de-sac and should therefore be quiet. Facilities for children. Open all the year. 20 rooms, all with hot and cold water. Bed and breakfast, 30s.–32s. 6d. Week, 13–14 gn.

SAVOY PARK HOTEL (Ayr 66112). Another delightful hotel with pleasant main rooms and comfortable bedrooms. A large garden runs down to the sea front. Putting green. Open all the year. 19 rooms, all with hot and cold water. Bed and breakfast, 30s.–35s. Day, 47s. 6d.–55s.

Alloway

BURNS MONUMENT HOTEL (Alloway 218). Ideally placed for a Burns pilgrimage. The River Doon, where there is salmon fishing, runs through the hotel garden; golf near by. Lounges, bar. Open all the year. 7 rooms, all with hot and cold water. Bed and breakfast, 30s. Day, 45s.

Prestwick

LINKS HOTEL (Prestwick 77792). This hotel stands in nearly two acres of grounds, overlooking the sea and adjoining the golf course. Children are welcome and they can reach both beach and bathing pool quickly from the hotel. Spacious main rooms; kitchen garden; central heating. Open all the year. 12 rooms, all with hot and cold water. Bed and breakfast, from 30s. Day, from 42s. 6d.

PARKSTONE HOTEL (Prestwick 77286). Well situated and should be a good place for family holidays. Open April–October. 18 rooms, all with hot and cold water. Bed and breakfast, 27s.–31s. Week, 12–14 gn.

Troon

MARINE HOTEL (Troon 980). Large de-luxe hotel close to the sea and golf courses. Bar, modern restaurant, spacious lounges, dancing, tennis courts. Lift; central heating throughout. Children are catered for, with a large indoor recreation room. Open all the year. 80 rooms, some with private bath; some suites. Bed and breakfast, 50s. Day, from 75s. Plus 10 per cent service.

SUN COURT HOTEL (Troon 1066). In extensive grounds with golf courses on three sides and the sandy beach within 200 yards, this is a really delightful place. The food is good, the cellars well stocked, the prices reasonable. Special meals for children. Lounges, bar. Open all the year. 12 rooms, some with bath. Bed and breakfast, from 30s. Week, from 15 gn. Plus 10 per cent service.

Skelmorlie

MANOR PARK HOTEL (Wemyss Bay 3232). A charming, luxurious hotel, in an elevated position in lovely gardens, with views of the coast. Main rooms decorated in exceptionally good taste; excellent flower arrangements. Open all the year. 12 rooms, some with bath. Bed and breakfast, 38s. Week, 18–20 gn.

Glasgow

Scotland's largest city, GLASGOW is also the most important commercial and industrial centre in the country. It is not generally considered to be a holiday place, but holiday-makers passing through could use it as a base for day excursions to the Ayrshire coast, Loch Lomond, the Trossachs and Perth; steamer trips on the Clyde give an interesting view of the extensive shipyards.

In the city itself, the art gallery has one of the finest municipal collections in Britain, and there are the Gothic cathedral and neo-Gothic university, as well as various museums; also plenty of shops and entertainments.

London, *394 miles*; Edinburgh, *44 miles*; Ayr, *33 miles*; Perth, *61 miles*; Oban, *93 miles*; Inverness, *168 miles.*

Rail. Buses. Steamer and air services.

Hotels

CENTRAL HOTEL, Gordon Street, C.1 (Central 9680). At the Central Station. Large, well-appointed and comfortable. The Malmaison Restaurant is notable and worth the expense; meals, à la carte. Lift, TV, central heating. 240 rooms, all with hot and cold water and some with bath. Bed and breakfast, 70s.–95s. Plus 10 per cent service.

MORE'S HOTEL, India Street, C.2 (Central 2641). Agreeable, not too large hotel with a sound reputation and good amenities. Five minutes' walk from the heart of the city. Restaurant; meals, à la carte. Lounges, bar, TV, lift. 72 rooms, all with hot and cold water and a few with bath. Bed and breakfast, 55s.–67s. 6d. Plus 10 per cent service.

MACDONALD HOTEL, Eastwood Toll, Giffnock (Giffnock 2225). On the southern outskirts of Glasgow, about 15 minutes from the city centre and half an hour from the coast. New hotel with classy modern décor; up-to-date facilities. Children catered for and cots and high-chairs provided. Open all the year. 37 rooms, all with hot and cold water and some with bath or shower. Bed and breakfast, from 47s. 6d; lunch, from 12s. 6d.; dinner, from 17s. 6d. Plus 10 per cent service.

BUCHANAN ARMS HOTEL, Drymen, Stirlingshire (Drymen 310). In the country about 18 miles north of Glasgow. Excellent, high-class hotel known for its good food. Visitors with the time and the money might choose to stay here rather than in the city. There are views of the hills; fishing and golf are available in the vicinity, and Loch Lomond is only four miles away. Open all the year. 27 rooms, all with hot and cold water and some with bath. Bed and breakfast, from 37s. 6d. Day, from 55s. Plus 10 per cent service.

Restaurants

RESTAURANT ROGANO, 11 Exchange Place, C.1 (Central 5677). Excellent fish restaurant and one of the best known eating-places in Glasgow. Long and varied menu, not confined to fish dishes. Prices not too high. Advisable to book. Closed on Sundays.

RESTAURANT ONE-O-ONE, 101 Hope Street, C.2 (Central 7101). Reasonably-priced restaurant with good service. In the city centre and useful for an evening meal before or after the theatre. Good lunch and dinner menus at 13s. 6d. and 17s. 6d. respectively; also wide choice à la carte. Dinner-dance every Saturday. Closed on Sundays.

GUY'S RESTAURANT, 188 Hope Street, C.2 (Douglas 3568). Similar in style to the One-o-One. Food and service of a reasonable standard; very good wine cellar. Closed on Sundays.

RESTAURANT FERRARI, 10 Sauchiehall Street, C.2 (Douglas 8414). An Italian family business, this is a praiseworthy, unassuming restaurant. The seating is comfortable, the service attentive and the food first-class, particularly the Continental dishes. Elderly Glasgow businessmen who pride themselves on their taste bring their clients here. Three-course lunch 10s.; four-course dinner 16s.; also à la carte. Closed on Sundays.

THE GAY GORDON, 21 Royal Exchange Square, C.1 (City 3040). Centrally placed, smallish and expensive. Heavy Caledonian décor and double-whisky heartiness. Some sophistication in the evenings, when a band plays for dancing. Business lunch, 12s. 6d.; pre-theatre dinner, 15s.; also à la carte (minimum charge after 7 p.m., 17s. 6d.). Advisable to book. Closed on Sundays.

Isle of Arran

One of the islands comprising the county of Bute, Arran lies out in the Firth of Clyde between the Ayrshire coast and the protecting arm of the Kintyre peninsula. It has been likened to a miniature Scotland, providing as it does examples of many of the features to be found on the mainland—mountains, glens and moorland, burns, lochs, rocks and sandy bays.

It is very much a holiday island; facilities are varied and well organised but in no way commercialised. The rugged coast and country have excellent walking, climbing and fishing, and the resorts offer all the bathing, golf, tennis, boat trips, excursions and other entertainments demanded by families at the seaside.

On the east coast, BRODICK, the principal port and resort, has a fine setting of encircling mountains, and three of Arran's loveliest glens converge on the bay. Beyond the town are two excellent sandy beaches, with shallow water safe for children; behind lie golf courses and woods.

Travelling northwards from Brodick, one passes through the unspoilt districts of Corrie and Sannox, where whitewashed cottages are scattered along the shore beneath the hills. In the northern corner of the island is LOCHRANZA, a village quite different in character from others on Arran. It is set round a bay of sand and pebbles, green hills sloping up from the water to give it a pastoral appearance, and there are the dominating ruins of a seventeenth-century castle.

Turning down the rocky west coast, the road follows the sea closely, through peaceful hamlets in wild and beautiful country. MACHRIE, on wide Machrie Bay, has beaches of sand and shingle and some of the best river fishing on the island; BLACKWATERFOOT, a few miles beyond, offers golfing and pony-trekking.

In the south of Arran, KILMORY gives its name to a district of moors and agricultural land which includes the villages of Lagg, Sliddery, Corriecravie and Bennan. KILDONAN, the smallest of the island's resorts, stands on a headland looking across to the islet of Pladda and its lighthouse. Beyond Dippin Head, is WHITING BAY, a popular resort with a mixed sand and shingle beach and a wooded background. LAMLASH, another favourite holiday centre, lies on the sand beach of Lamlash Bay, guarded by the 1,000-foot peak of Holy Island.

Brodick–Lochranza, *14 miles*; Brodick–Whiting Bay, *8 miles*; Brodick–Kilmory, *10 miles*.

Steamer services: Ardrossan, Fairlie Pier, Gourock and Wemyss Bay–Brodick. Car ferries: Ardrossan and Fairlie Pier–Brodick. Buses.

County: Bute.

Hotels   Brodick

DOUGLAS HOTEL (Brodick 5). Overlooking the bay and close to the landing-stage, this hotel offers comfortable rooms, good food, and a large lawn. Open all the year. 30 rooms, all with hot and cold water. Bed and breakfast, 30s.–32s. 6d. Week, 14–15 gn.

KINGSLEY HOTEL (Brodick 26). Congenial hotel with good food, situated on the sea front, within five minutes' walk of the pier and beach. Unlicensed. Open Easter–October. 21 rooms, all with hot and cold water. Bed and breakfast, 25s. Week, $9\frac{1}{2}$–$12\frac{1}{2}$ gn.

Lochranza

LOCHRANZA HOTEL (Lochranza 223). Well-situated "pub" type of hotel. 20 rooms, about half with hot and cold water. Bed and breakfast, 22s. 6d.–25s. 6d. Week, 8–11 gn.

FAIRHAVEN BOARD RESIDENCE, Catacol, by Lochranza (Lochranza 237). Agreeable guesthouse with terraced lawn descending to the road and the shingle beach. The standard is high, and guests return year after year. Excellent sea fishing. Unlicensed. 8 rooms, with hot and cold water. Week, 7 gn.

Machrie

MACHRIE PRIVATE HOTEL (Machrie Bay 23). In a rural district, backed by sweeping hills and close to a shingle beach on a sheltered cove. Unlicensed. Open Easter–October. 11 rooms, some with hot and cold water. Bed and breakfast, from 21s. Week, from 8 gn.

Blackwaterfoot

KINLOCH HOTEL (Shiskine 286). Family hotel by the sea, with garden, games room, lounges, bar, TV. Open all the year. 38 rooms, with hot and cold water. Bed and breakfast, 21s. Day, 30s.–33s. Plus 5 per cent service.

Kilmory

LAGG INN (Sliddery 55). In attractive gardens with tall palms. Furnishings are comfortable and the décor plain but gay. Coach parties do call at the hotel, but none the less this is an excellent place for a stay. Open March–October. 12 rooms, with hot and cold water. Bed and breakfast, 20s.–45s. Week, from 11 gn.

Kildonan

KILDONAN HOTEL (Kildonan 207). Large hotel standing on its own at the tip of the headland, close to the sea and a sandy beach backed by fields. The hotel has its own tennis court and putting green and there is golf near by. Open all the year. 31 rooms, most with hot and cold water. Bed and breakfast, 21s.–23s. Week, 10–12 gn.

Whiting Bay

WHITING BAY HOTEL (Whiting Bay 247). Comfortable, well-heated hotel overlooking the bay and the Firth of Clyde and about five minutes from the steamer pier. Tennis courts in the grounds; bowling green adjacent. Open all the year. 20 rooms, all with hot and cold water. Bed and breakfast, 25s. Week, 11–14 gn.

Lamlash

WHITE HOUSE HOTEL (Lamlash 212). Former home of the Duchess

of Hamilton, this seventeenth-century house stands in magnificent wooded grounds overlooking the sea. A modern wing has been added, and it is now a pleasant if rather old-fashioned hotel. Open all the year. 17 rooms, all with hot and cold water. Bed and breakfast, from 25s. Week, $9\frac{1}{2}$–$11\frac{1}{2}$ gn.

WESTERN HIGHLANDS
AND ISLANDS

Loch Fyne

This loch stretches for some 40 miles from just beyond the little town of INVERARAY to the Sound of Bute, between the Island of Bute and the shore of the Kintyre peninsula.

Inveraray, in wooded country near the head of the loch, is a royal burgh and the capital of Argyll. Inveraray Castle, seat of the Duke of Argyll, head of Clan Campbell, is open daily. The town is uninteresting, but a centre for tourists. Some miles further down the northern shore is the tiny LOCHGAIR inlet.

Near the mouth of the loch, TARBERT is a holiday resort and the centre of the Loch Fyne herring industry. There are sands for bathing; golf, and walking in the wooded hills that rise from Loch Fyne and West Loch Tarbert.

Edinburgh–Inveraray, *102 miles*; Oban–Inveraray, *39 miles*; Inveraray–Tarbert, *38 miles*.

Railway stations: Dalmally (for Inveraray); Gourock (for Tarbert). Steamers to Glasgow, Ardrishaig, Inner Hebrides. Buses. County: Argyll.

Hotels   Inveraray

GEORGE HOTEL (Inveraray 2111). In the town; suitable for overnight stops. Lounge, TV. Guests met at Dalmally station on request. Open all the year. 23 rooms, all with hot and cold water. Bed and breakfast, 30s.–32s. 6d. Week, from 13 gn.

Tarbert

STONEFIELD CASTLE HOTEL (Tarbert 207). Large country-house hotel in a beautiful park on Loch Fyne, a few miles outside Tarbert. Rare shrubs grow in the wooded grounds, and inside the house the flowers are exquisitely arranged. This would be a place for complete peace and calm in real comfort; it seems to appeal particularly to older people. Panelled dining-room, spacious drawing-room overlooking the loch, library, cocktail bar, TV, table tennis. In the grounds are tennis court, putting green and clock golf, and there is a sandy bathing beach with shallow water safe for children; also yacht anchorage. Garages. Own farm produce. No dogs. Open end March–end October. 24 rooms, all with hot and cold water, some with bath. Bed and breakfast, 35s.–40s. Week, 17–21 gn.

Lochgair

LOCHGAIR HOTEL (Lochgair 213). Tastefully and comfortably furnished hotel on the shores of the loch. The owners are charming, the food well-cooked and served. Open all the year. 18 rooms, all with hot and cold water. Bed and breakfast, from 25s. Week, 12–15 gn.

Crinan and Loch Awe

On the coast not far from Loch Fyne and Loch Awe, CRINAN is an engaging little village in splendid surroundings at the western end of the Crinan Canal. This canal, nine miles long with 15 locks, was built from Ardrishaig at the end of the eighteenth century to enable ships to reach the open sea from Loch Fyne, avoiding the stormy Mull of Kintyre. This place would be ideal for a quiet sailing or fishing holiday, but a car would be essential. Across the bay is Duntroon Castle, one of the oldest in Scotland and still inhabited by the original family owners, the Clan Malcolm.

Twenty-three miles long and about a mile wide, LOCH AWE is a most attractive inland loch, the shores bordered by woods and hills and the water dotted with islands. At its southern extremity is the little angling centre of FORD; the wilder northern end is dominated by Ben Cruachan mountain.

Inveraray–Crinan, *30 miles*; Oban–Crinan, *35 miles*; Crinan–Ford, *10 miles*; Ford–Dalmally, *28 miles*.
Railway stations: Dalmally, Oban, Taynuilt.
County: Argyll.

Hotels   Crinan

CRINAN HOTEL, by Lochgilphead (Crinan 215). Good-class hotel
with bright décor and modern comforts. It stands beside the
canal and yacht basin and sailing is a special attraction. The hotel
has facilities for those bringing their own dinghies; boats can
also be hired. Lounges, bar, TV, central heating. Rock garden
and terrace. Open all the year. 20 rooms, all with hot and cold
water, a few with bath. Bed and breakfast, 35s.–45s. Week, 16–21
gn. Plus 10 per cent service.

Loch Awe

FORD HOTEL, Ford, by Lochgilphead (Ford 203). Angling hotel
in the remote village at the southern end of Loch Awe. Salmon
and trout fishing in surrounding waters, walks in the hills and
woods, and boat trips on the loch. Bar, lounge. Guests will be
met at Oban, but a car is really a necessity here. Open March–
October. 12 rooms, with hot and cold water. Bed and breakfast,
26s. Week, 12 gn.

PORTSONACHAN HOTEL, by Dalmally, Lochaweside (Kilchrenan
224). In peaceful, beautiful surroundings on the north-eastern
shore of the loch, right by the water and looking across to hills
and mountains, this is a charming, well-kept hotel providing good
food, comfort and service. Salmon and trout fishing; boats
available for cruises and picnics; hill ponies for riding. Country
dances on Saturday nights. Lounges, bar, garden, table tennis.
Guests met at Dalmally station (10 miles) on request, but a car
is advisable as the hotel is isolated and not on a bus route. Open
March 15–October 15. 25 rooms, all with hot and cold water.
Dinner, bed and breakfast, from 2½ gn. Week, from 17½ gn.

INVERINAN LODGE, by Taynuilt (Kilchrenan 204). This lodge, on
the western shore, near the head of the loch, combines the informal atmosphere of a Highland shooting lodge with the comfort
of a small country hotel. Sun lounge with views down the loch
and of Ben Cruachan. Good salmon and trout fishing (boats
available), riding, stalking and shooting; also walking, climbing,

boating. Guests met at Taynuilt station (12 miles) on request.
Open March–October. 9 rooms, all with hot and cold water.
Week, 11–13 gn. Sports extra.

Riding holidays with instruction are held from March–July
and September–October. Week, 15–16 gn. (inclusive).

Kilmelford, Easdale

The small resort of KILMELFORD is at the head of Loch Melfort,
on the coast to the south of OBAN.

Just to the west is the island of Seil, the narrow straits being
spanned by the old stone Clachan Bridge—whimsically called the
only bridge across the Atlantic Ocean. The little seaside village
of EASDALE, on Seil, faces the tiny island of the same name,
reached by ferry. There is fishing, boating and walking in peace
and isolation.

Oban–Kilmelford, *15 miles*; Oban–Easdale, *16 miles*.
Railway station: Oban. Buses.
County: Argyll.

Hotels   Kilmelford

CUILFAIL HOTEL (Kilmelford 204). Isolated hotel on the coast
road south of Oban. Well placed for exploring the wild and
beautiful countryside by car. Pretty garden; central heating.
Trout fishing free to guests; boats for hire. 18 rooms, all with
hot and cold water. Dinner, bed and breakfast, 40s. Week, 14 gn.

Easdale

INSHAIG PARK HOTEL (Balvicar 256). This hotel stands by itself on
a slope above the road, overlooking the islands. It is simple but
pleasant, and the annexe is particularly attractive. Farm produce.
10 rooms, with hot and cold water. Bed and breakfast, 25s.–30s.
Week, from 12 gn.

Oban

One of the main holiday centres of the west coast of Scotland, OBAN attracts those who like a town as a base for touring, rather than the isolated mountain or loch-side hotel more usual in the Highlands. It is an attractive town, beautifully situated on a bay, sloping down to the active port, with fine views across to the Inner Hebrides.

A tempting variety of excursions are possible into the magnificent country inland and to the islands, and the car-less would find the organised coach and boat trips a great boon. There is also walking, bathing from Ganavan Sands two miles outside the town, sailing, water-skiing, fishing, golf, tennis.

London, *487 miles*; Edinburgh, *125 miles*; Fort William, *49 miles* (using ferry).

Rail. Buses. Steamers.

County: Argyll.

Hotels

GREAT WESTERN HOTEL (Oban 3101). Large, stately hotel at the northern end of the promenade overlooking the islands and near the pier and station. Comfort and spaciousness are combined with efficient service and good if unexciting food. Trips are arranged in the hotel boat. Lift; dancing, bar, lounges, games room. Open May–October. 82 rooms, all with hot and cold water, many with bath. Day, 52s. 6d.–59s. 6d. Plus 10 per cent service.

MARINE HOTEL (Oban 2211). Comfortable, modern hotel, centrally situated on the sea front, with views of the islands. Good food in the attractive dining-room. Lift; bar, central heating. Open April–October. 38 rooms, all with hot and cold water. Dinner, bed and breakfast, 47s. 6d.–62s. 6d. Week, 16–22½ gn.

ALEXANDRA HOTEL (Oban 2381). This hotel has a good, sunny and quiet position on the esplanade. Efficiently run and remarkably inexpensive for what is offered. Airy lounge, sun lounge, bar, recreation room. Lift; garage. No dogs. Open April–October. 61 rooms, all with hot and cold water, a few with bath. Bed and breakfast, 36s.–42s. Day, 48s.–57s.

KING'S KNOLL HOTEL (Oban 2536). On the main road out of town, overlooking the bay; good amenities, but rather unexciting food. The owners do all they can to help guests. TV, central heating. Pony-trekking holidays between April and September. Open all the year. 21 comfortable rooms, arranged with taste, all with hot and cold water. Dinner, bed and breakfast, 37s. 6d. Day, 48s.

REGENT HOTEL (Oban 2341). Large, central hotel on the sea front close to the pier and station. Friendly service and good food. Lift; lounges. Open May to end-September. 39 rooms, all with hot and cold water. Bed and breakfast, 37s. 6d. Day, from 54s.

Appin, Onich

On the road northwards from Oban to Ballachulish and FORT WILLIAM, the district of Appin, described in R. L. Stevenson's "Kidnapped", lies between Loch Creran and Loch Linnhe.

PORT APPIN is a most inviting, peaceful little place of a few stone cottages, off the main road on an inlet of Loch Linnhe. There are views over the surrounding lochs and islands and the majestic countryside, with pleasant walks as well as boating and fishing.

Well situated on the shores of Loch Linnhe, ONICH is just to the north of the Ballachulish Ferry (continuous service, but congested in summer), which crosses the mouth of Loch Leven. There is walking and climbing in the area, and this should be a good centre for those with a car.

Oban–Port Appin, *25 miles*; Port Appin–Ballachulish, *17 miles*; Onich–Fort William, *10 miles*.

Railway stations: Appin, Ballachulish, Fort William. Buses.
Steamers: Oban–Fort William steamer will call at Appin by
arrangement.
Counties: Argyll (Appin); Inverness-shire (Onich).

Hotels   Port Appin

AIRDS HOTEL (Appin 236). A delightful hotel, originally an old
ferry inn, comfortable and arranged with taste. Lounge, tiny bar.
Sea and loch fishing; boats for hire. Open Easter–October. 17
rooms, with hot and cold water. Dinner, bed and breakfast,
37s. 6d. Week, 12 gn.

Onich

LOCH LEVEN HOTEL, North Ballachulish, Onich, by Fort William
(Onich 236). Modest but attractive hotel on the main road by
the ferry. The proprietress does her best to make guests welcome,
and many return each year. Lounges; garden; garage. Dairy
farm attached. No dogs. Open all the year. 10 rooms, all with
hot and cold water and electric fires. Bed and breakfast, 22s. 6d–
28s. 6d. Week, 9–11 gn.

ALLT-NAN-ROS HOTEL, Onich, by Fort William (Onich 201, 210).
Excellent hotel in its own grounds, with views southwards across
the loch to the hills. The owners are very kind, and guests return
year after year. Lounges, bar, central heating, putting green.
Open Easter–mid October. 30 rooms, all with hot and cold water.
Bed and breakfast, 30s. Week, 14–16 gn. Plus 10 per cent service.

ONICH HOTEL, Onich, by Fort William (Onich 214). Comfortable,
with food of a good standard; well placed beside the loch, the
garden going down to the water. Open Easter to mid-October.
17 rooms, all with hot and cold water. Bed and breakfast, 34s. 6d.
Week, 14½ gn.

Fort William

At the head of Loch Linnhe, beneath Ben Nevis and at the
western end of the Great Glen, FORT WILLIAM is a good centre

from which to explore the Western Highlands and Islands. The town itself is lacking in attraction but is lively enough and has plenty of holiday amenities.

London, *509 miles*; Edinburgh, *146 miles*; Oban, *68 miles*; Inverness, *66 miles*.

Rail. Buses. Steamers.

County: Inverness-shire.

Hotels

ALEXANDRA HOTEL (Fort William 26). Comfortable and well run, this hotel is close to the railway station and pier and has views of the loch and hills. Helpful staff. Lounges, bar, garden. 35 rooms, all with hot and cold water. Bed and breakfast, from 35s. Week, 16–18 gn.

WEST END HOTEL (Fort William 53). Modernised hotel with all comforts and good food. On the main road overlooking the loch and mountains and close to the town centre. Open Easter–October. 30 rooms, all with hot and cold water. Bed and breakfast, 32s. 6d. Week, 14–15 gn.

CROIT-ANNA MOTEL (Fort William 3). Modern motel two miles outside Fort William on Loch Linnhe side. Well furnished, with good food, comfort and service. Open all the year. 18 double rooms, all with hot and cold water. Dinner, bed and breakfast, 42s. Week, 14 gn. Plus 10 per cent service.

Morar, Mallaig

For romantic associations and grandeur of scenery the "Road to the Isles" between FORT WILLIAM and the sea would be hard to beat. Both road and railway run west from Fort William, through sombre Glenfinnan (where the monument commemorates the raising of Bonnie Prince Charlie's standard during the '45 Rebellion), to meet the sea at Lochailort and continue up the coast through Arisaig, MORAR and MALLAIG. Land and sea views are magnificent, the wild mountains, lochs, islands and sea brought to life by the everchanging light.

At Arisaig, a few buildings are scattered by the low rugged shore. Morar, a few miles beyond and no larger, is situated where the Morar river flows down from Loch Morar to the sea. The white sands of Morar, edging the river mouth and the rocky coast on either side, provide wonderful bathing beaches when the tide and the weather are right. You can walk in solitude by the deep waters of Loch Morar, where the views are very beautiful, particularly looking towards the high peaks at the eastern end.

Mallaig, at the end of the peninsula, is a lively small fishing port facing the Isle of Skye and surrounded by lonely, impressive loch and mountain country. Regular steamers cross to SKYE, and there are a variety of other boat trips and rewarding walks for the energetic.

Fort William–Mallaig, *48 miles*; Morar–Mallaig, *3 miles*.
Railway stations: Mallaig, Morar, Arisaig. Buses. Steamers.
County: Inverness-shire.

Hotels   Morar

MORAR HOTEL (Mallaig 37). Ideal for those seeking peace. It overlooks the coast, with the sands near by and wild country all round. Children welcome. Open April–October. 30 rooms, all with hot and cold water. Bed and breakfast, from 28s. 6d. Week, 13–15 gn.

Mallaig

WEST HIGHLAND HOTEL (Mallaig 10). The largest and leading hotel, in an elevated position in the village, facing the harbour and looking across to Skye, Rhum and Eigg. Rather old-fashioned, but comfortable and pleasing. Open all the year. 32 rooms, all with hot and cold water. Bed and breakfast, 30s. Week, 15 gn.

MARINE HOTEL (Mallaig 17). Rather quaint little place right in the village, above shops and the bank; small garden below.

Good service. 20 rooms, all with hot and cold water. Bed and breakfast, 27s. 6d.–30s. Week, from 13 gn.

PRIMROSE BOARD RESIDENCE (Mallaig 43). This neat little cottage surrounded by flowers makes a simple but agreeable guesthouse. On the bay on the village edge. Unlicensed. Open Easter–end September. 7 rooms, with hot and cold water. High tea, bed and breakfast, 21s.

Spean Bridge, Invergarry, Tomdoun

North of Fort William on the way to dark, beautiful Loch Lochy, SPEAN BRIDGE is a stopping place on the main road through the Great Glen. Beyond, at INVERGARRY on Loch Oich, a road branches westwards towards the coast, passing along Loch Garry and through Highland country of moors, hills, rocks and rushing rivers. Loch Garry is very lovely, and a secondary road leads to TOMDOUN at its farther end, isolated in wild, open country.

Fort William–Spean Bridge, *10 miles*; Spean Bridge–Invergarry, *15 miles*; Invergarry–Tomdoun, *10 miles*.

Railway station: Spean Bridge.

County: Inverness-shire.

Hotels   Spean Bridge

SPEAN BRIDGE HOTEL (Spean Bridge 250). Small, homely hotel on the main road, convenient for overnight stops. Garage. Open all the year. 20 rooms, all with hot and cold water. Bed and breakfast, 30s.–35s. Week, 14–16 gn.

LETTERFINLAY LODGE HOTEL (Invergloy 211). On the shores of Loch Lochy, in a beautiful setting in its own grounds between the road and the water, this is an agreeable family hotel ideal for a peaceful Highland holiday. Trout fishing for guests; salmon and sea trout fishing and stalking by arrangement. Lounges, sun lounge, bar. 15 rooms, all with hot and cold water. Dinner, bed and breakfast, 40s. Week, £14.

Invergarry

GLENGARRY CASTLE HOTEL (Invergarry 254). Secluded country house standing in a park with gardens descending gently to Loch Oich. Suited to seekers after rest and comfort, and to families. Tastefully furnished; log fires in public rooms, central heating. Trout fishing, tennis court, boating. Restricted licence. Open Easter–October. 24 rooms, all with hot and cold water. Bed and breakfast, 26s.–28s. 6d. Week, 13–14 gn.

Also three furnished cottages in the grounds. (1) 1 bedroom, £9 week; (2) 2 bedrooms, £12; (3) 3 bedrooms, £14.

INVERGARRY HOTEL (Invergarry 206). By the river in Glen Garry, not far from Loch Oich, this is a good sportsman's hotel with a friendly atmosphere. Salmon and trout fishing; shooting and deer-stalking by arrangement. Guests met at Spean Bridge (18 miles) or Inverness (42 miles) on request. Open April to mid-November. 14 rooms, all with hot and cold water. Bed and breakfast, from 25s. Week, from 15½ gn.

Tomdoun

TOMDOUN HOTEL (Tomdoun 214). An austere fishing inn in beautiful, remote country on the shores of Loch Garry. Salmon and trout fishing, although the salmon have been affected by a hydro-electric scheme. 14 rooms, all with hot and cold water. Bed and breakfast, 30s.–34s. Week, 14–16 gn.

Loch Duich

Back on the main road to Kyle of Lochalsh, the scenery is striking but severe, with bleak hills and moorland. This is one of the main routes to the Isle of Skye and busy in summer.

It could be you, set down among,
The lochs, the glens, the heather,
It could be you, with rod or gun,
All careless of the weather.
If you enjoy a great outdoors,
Your only grouse will be on moors,
So book your ticket there today,
Fly BEA and Scots Wha Hae.

 EUROPE'S FOREMOST AIRLINE

As one passes through Glen Shiel and approaches the Kintail district around LOCH DUICH, the country suddenly becomes more gentle, with trees and rhododendrons, fields sloping down to the water, and little farms and cottages. There are wonderful views of the loch and mountains (including the Five Sisters of Kintail), and much of this fine country belongs to the National Trust for Scotland.

In lovely surroundings where Loch Duich meets Loch Long and Loch Alsh, is the tiny village of DORNIE, and near by Eilean Donan Castle juts into the water, joined to the shore by a causeway (open daily except Sunday).

Throughout this district there is fishing, boating, walking and climbing.

Fort William–Dornie, *68 miles*; Dornie–Kyle of Lochalsh, *11 miles*.

Railway stations: Kyle of Lochalsh, Stromeferry. Buses.

County: Ross-shire.

Hotels　　　　　　　　　　　　　　Loch Duich

KINTAIL LODGE HOTEL, Glenshiel, by Kyle (Glenshiel 205). Attractive hotel in a pretty garden at the head of Loch Duich, with views of the water and mountains of Kintail. The interior is decorated with taste and originality by the young owners, who look after their guests well and provide good home cooking. Climbers and naturalists catered for; also salmon and trout fishing; ponies and boats available. Open Easter–October. 12 double rooms, all with hot and cold water. Week, 12 gn.

Dornie

DORNIE HOTEL (Dornie 205). Well-kept small inn on the main road. Open from Easter. 16 rooms, all with hot and cold water. Bed and breakfast, 32s. 6d. Week, 16½ gn.

LOCH DUICH HOTEL, Ardelve, Kyle of Lochalsh (Dornie 213). This comfortable hotel has a perfect situation at the meeting point of the three lochs, facing Eilean Donan Castle. Children catered for; games room, laundry and drying facilities, lounge, bar. Trout and sea fishing; boats for hire. Open all the year. 18 rooms

E　　　　　　　　　　　　65

and 4 in annexe, all with hot and cold water. Bed and breakfast, 30s.–35s. Week, from 15 gn.

Kyle of Lochalsh

The BALMACARA estate (now the property of the National Trust) along Loch Alsh between Dornie and Kyle has beautiful, smiling country and views over the sea to Skye. Equally beautifully situated at the mouth of the loch and looking across the narrow straits to Skye, KYLE OF LOCHALSH is very much a centre for reaching the surrounding coast, lochs and islands.

London–Kyle of Lochalsh, *587 miles*; Edinburgh, *225 miles*; Fort William, *79 miles*.

Railway station: Kyle of Lochalsh. Car and passenger ferry to Skye; other steamers. Buses.

County: Ross-shire.

Hotels   Balmacara

BALMACARA HOTEL (Balmacara 213). Congenial, unassuming hotel on the road along Balmacara Bay, facing the Cuillins of Skye. Fishing. Open all the year. 23 rooms, all with hot and cold water. Bed and breakfast, 25s. 6d.–32s. 6d. Week, 10–14 gn.

Kyle of Lochalsh

LOCHALSH HOTEL (Kyle 4202). Top-class hotel, efficiently run by British Transport. On the loch beside the ferry, it has splendid views of Skye, and there are pine woods and moorland behind. As well as comfort, the hotel provides extremely good food, served in the restaurant overlooking the loch. Central heating throughout. Open all the year. 37 rooms, all with hot and cold water, some with bath. Bed and breakfast, 45s.–73s. Week, 20–25 gn. Plus 10 per cent service.

Loch Carron District

Northwards from Kyle of Lochalsh, travellers cross Loch Carron by the Strome Ferry (fare 10s.; no service on Sunday) and continue through bare, desolate country to Achnasheen.

From the north shore of Loch Carron a side road leads through wild country to the tiny village of SHIELDAIG on a sea inlet of Loch Torridon, where there is walking and fishing in the peace and solitude of the magnificent surroundings. The striking Torridon mountains can be seen to the north and the village of Torridon at the head of the loch is accessible by boat also by car, on completion of the new shore road.

Kyle of Lochalsh–Achnasheen, *40 miles*; Strathcarron–Shieldaig, *18 miles*.

Railway station: Strathcarron. Buses. Boats.

County: Ross-shire.

Hotel   Shieldaig

TIGH-AN-EILEAN, Shieldaig, by Strathcarron (Shieldaig 201). A delightful, small guesthouse, on the loch with excellent views. Beautifully furnished and decorated, and exceptional food for such a remote spot. Library with a wide selection of books. Good sea fishing. Children welcome. Unlicensed. Open all the year. 5 rooms, all with hot and cold water. Bed and breakfast, 25s. 6d. Week, 12 gn.

Isle of Islay

Most southerly of the Hebrides, Islay is some 25 miles long and 20 miles broad and is separated from its near neighbour, Jura, by a narrow sound. It enjoys a comparatively mild climate and attractive scenery and has for industries, agriculture, fishing and distilleries. There is no encircling road, but roads connect the main villages. Most visitors, however, will want to explore on foot, for there is much of botanical interest and a wide variety of unusual birds are to be seen.

Situated on the Sound of Islay facing Jura, little PORT ASKAIG has a pier for steamers from the mainland and other islands. It offers excellent fishing and pleasant walks.

On the western side of the island, there are gentle hills and open valleys, trees and meadows—covered in spring with acres of wild flowers. Past the head of Loch Gruinart and inland Loch Gorm lies Saligo Bay, on the coast. Here grass comes down to the sand, a stream flows into the sea, and strange rock formations point northwards like guardian cannon.

Similar beaches can be found to the south at Machir Bay, Kilchiaran Bay and Lossit Bay, all on the outer edge of the Rhinns Peninsula—but there are rollers and bathing can be dangerous.

Large Loch Indaal forms the inner side of the Rhinns Peninsula, with more expanses of sand skirting the water, with good opportunities for the bird-watcher. PORT CHARLOTTE is on a rocky stretch of the coast. BOWMORE, on the eastern shore of the loch, is a fishing village noted for its curious circular parish church of Kilmarrow, constructed in the mid-eighteenth century.

Laggan Bay to the south has an immense stretch of sand providing good bathing and surfing. The island's airport borders the lower half of the bay, and here sheep graze until turned off at the approach of an aircraft. Beyond is the Machrie golf course.

PORT ELLEN in the south-west of the island is Islay's chief port, its simple main street and promenade following the bay round to a sandy beach. Famous for distilleries that produce single-malt Highland whiskies by the old-fashioned pot-still method.

Port Askaig–Port Charlotte, *23 miles*; Port Askaig–Port Ellen, *20 miles*.

Steamer services: Tarbert–Port Askaig, Tarbert–Port Ellen (cars carried by arrangement). Airport. Buses.

County: Argyll.

Hotels   Port Askaig

PORT ASKAIG HOTEL (Port Askaig 205). Close to the landing-stage, with wooded slopes behind, this charming small hotel provides unassuming comfort and simple food. Guests would meet the local people who frequent the little bar. There is salmon, trout and sea fishing and a special welcome for anglers, as the proprietors themselves fish and are glad to indicate the best spots. A car would be an advantage, but the hotel has a car for hire. Open all the year. 10 rooms, all with hot and cold water. Week, from 13 gn.

Port Charlotte

PORT CHARLOTTE HOTEL (Port Charlotte 219). A hotel full of atmosphere, in the village, close to the sea. Lounges, and a "nautical" bar with views of the bay from portholes. Furnishings in good taste, fitted carpets. Open all the year. 12 rooms, all with hot and cold water. Week, 12 gn.

Bowmore

IMPERIAL HOTEL (Bowmore 261). Modest hotel pleasantly situated on a little square; some rooms face westwards over the sea. The proprietor will take guests on fishing trips. 5 rooms, with hot and cold water. Bed and breakfast, from 22s. 6d. Week, from 9 gn.

Port Ellen

WHITE HART HOTEL (Port Ellen 11). A delightful hotel on the little promenade just outside the town. Good food is served in the dining-room facing the sea, and there is a pleasant lounge with open fire. The proprietors will arrange fishing. 27 rooms, tastefully and cheerfully decorated, all with hot and cold water. Bed and breakfast, from 22s. 6d. Week, from 12 gn.

ARDVIEW HOTEL (Port Ellen 57). Modest hotel overlooking the sea and close to the landing-stage. Boats for loch and sea fishing; car for hire. Unlicensed. 9 plain rooms, most with hot and cold water. Bed and breakfast, from 21s. Day, 30s.

Isle of Mull

One of the Inner Hebrides, Mull lies just off the west coast opposite OBAN. Utterly wild, with the remote, even foreign, air that characterises much of the Western Highlands, the island would be perfect for a carefree, open-air holiday of walking, bathing, boating and fishing. The scenery is beautiful and varied, with rocky coast, mountains and moorland. Roads are few and often rough, but exploration can be done by car, bus and coach—or on foot.

TOBERMORY, the capital, is an engaging, active little port facing the mainland, its stone houses built along the quay and on the hillside. The bathing beach has been improved with imported sand; other summer holiday activities include sailing, golf and Highland events.

A good road runs south of Tobermory to SALEN on the Sound of Mull. The village is convenient for exploring, with walking and climbing around Ben More, the highest point on Mull.

The village of BUNESSAN—in the Ross of Mull, the south-western corner of the island—consists of a few whitewashed cottages lining the inner shore of a deep bay. Here you can walk and fish in solitude, and there is a sandy beach a short distance away; a few miles beyond, you can take the ferry from Fionphort across to Iona.

Up the west coast of Mull the country is bare and rugged, the road along Loch Na Keal following the sea closely beneath the sheer cliffs of Gribun Rocks.

Towards the north, the landscape becomes greener and is particularly pleasing around DERVAIG, a delightful small place on the sloping shores of Loch na Cuilce and Loch a' Chamhainn a few miles west of Tobermory. There is good hill walking, as well as climbing and fishing, in the district, and a sandy beach at Calgary Bay, four miles away.

Tobermory–Salen, *10 miles*; Tobermory–Bunessan, *43 miles*.

Steamer services: Oban–Tobermory via Salen; car ferry Oban–Craignure. Buses. Boats.

County: Argyll.

Hotels   Tobermory

WESTERN ISLES HOTEL (Tobermory 12). Good, if rather conventional, hotel in a commanding position above the harbour, with views over the bay. Well-appointed dining-room, lounge, sun lounge and terrace, bar, games room. Friendly proprietors; congenial atmosphere. Hard tennis court in the grounds; loch fishing from hotel boat. Open all the year. 50 rooms, all with hot and cold water, some with bath. Bed and breakfast, 30s. 6d–42s. 6d. Week, 13½–18 gn.

MISHNISH HOTEL (Tobermory 9). Small hotel on the front, close to the steamer landing stage, in an old house of low ceilings, narrow passages and polished wood. Run by the MacCleod family for four generations; personal attention and good, simple food. Hire-cars, boats for residents. Open all the year. 15 rooms, all with hot and cold water. Bed and breakfast, 18s. Day, 42s.

MACDONALD ARMS HOTEL (Tobermory 11). On the front at one end of Tobermory Bay, this is another old-established hotel. Plain, but acceptable and friendly. Open all the year. 10 rooms, with hot and cold water. Bed and breakfast, from 22s. 6d. Week, 12–14 gn.

STRONGARBH GUEST HOUSE (Tobermory 73). Set in a garden on the hill just outside Tobermory, in a beautiful situation with outstanding views. Simple home comforts. Boating parties arranged. Unlicensed. Open from March. 9 rooms, most with hot and cold water. Bed and breakfast, from 21s. Week, from 9½ gn.

Salen

GLENFORSA HOUSE HOTEL (Aros 77). Charming house with a welcoming atmosphere, in the country about two miles from Salen and close to the sea. There is a sheltered garden, and the River Forsa, skirting the grounds, has good trout and salmon fishing, available to guests. Boats for sea fishing; riding, deer-stalking by arrangement; bathing near by. Lounge with log fires.

Restricted licence. Open Easter to mid-October. 12 rooms, most with hot and cold water. Bed and breakfast, 22s. 6d.–25s. Week, 10½–13 gn.

Bunessan

ARGYLL ARMS HOTEL (Fionphort 215). This little hotel has been made most comfortable, neat and bright; views across sea and country. Open all the year. 8 rooms, with hot and cold water. Week, 12 gn.

Dervaig

BALLACHROY HOTEL (Dervaig 25). Attractive, homely hotel in the village, run by a farming family. Pleasant outlook. Farm produce; children welcome. Hotel car; boat for fishing on Loch Frisa. Open all the year. 5 rooms, with hot and cold water. Week, 10 gn.

Iona

This attractive little island, about 3 miles long and 1½ miles wide, is just off the south-west corner of Mull and reached by ferry from Fionphort (weather permitting) or by steamer from Oban or Tobermory.

Iona is treeless but green and pleasant, with a rocky coast and excellent sandy beaches; the climate is mild and dry. There are a few cottages in the village by the jetty, but no roads.

St Columba founded a monastery here when bringing Christianity to Scotland in the sixth century, and the remains of the cathedral and monastery (dating back to the eleventh and thirteenth centuries but largely rebuilt and still under restoration) are a place of pilgrimage.

Hotel

ST COLUMBA HOTEL (Iona 204). Neat hotel outside the village, near the cathedral. Some rooms overlook the sea. Open April–October, and usually fully booked in advance. 23 pleasant rooms, most with hot and cold water. Week, 12 gn.

Isle of Skye

The largest island of the Inner Hebrides (50 miles long) and the best known to tourists, Skye's individual atmosphere is enhanced by a romantic historical background. The Cuillins, a range of jagged black mountains, provide sensational scenery as well as opportunities for climbers.

The rocky coast is deeply indented by lochs, which break the island into a series of peninsulas, so that at no point is one more than five miles from the sea. Much of the country is wild and remote, but buses link most villages, and roads, although narrow, are adequate.

PORTREE, the capital, is a neat, bright little town built above the harbour on the bay, where steamers call and fishing boats shelter. Those seeking picnic spots, fishing and boating expeditions and golf are all catered for.

A few miles to the north, the Trotternish Peninsula forms the eastern side of the long Loch Snizort Beag. SKEABOST lies at the head of the loch and excursions can be made to beautiful Uig Bay and to the sandy beach at Staffin Bay. This district offers good fishing and shooting. It is full of memories of Flora MacDonald, including the site of her landing with Bonnie Prince Charlie in 1746, the house where she lived for much of her married life, and her grave.

EDINBANE, to the west, is surrounded by lonely moorland country at the head of Loch Greshornish, and a few miles further on is DUNVEGAN, where Dunvegan Castle, family seat of the MacLeods, is a popular tourist sight (open weekdays April–October). The main road turns down the west coast to skirt vast Loch Bracadale, and on a short arm of the loch lies STRUAN, set amid green hills.

SLIGACHAN is almost at the centre of Skye, isolated in splendid country at the head of Loch Sligachan. In the background are the Cuillins, and the one hotel is a centre for mountaineers (the hardier ones sometimes camp in remote Glen Brittle in the heart of the mountains), as well as for anglers and tourers by car.

Towards the lower part of the island there is one magnificent landscape after another, with comparatively rich areas along the east coast, which is protected by islands and by the mainland. BROADFORD village is scattered along wide Broadford Bay, where the water is clear and the rocky shore fringed by the characteristic, vividly-coloured seaweed—"the tangle of the Isles". Behind rise the neat, rounded outlines of the Red Hills.

The island's southernmost arm, the peninsula of Sleat, is known as the "Garden of Skye" and has more open, gentle countryside, with many trees and everywhere magnificent views of sea and hills. The road down the western shore passes through the hamlet of Isleornsay, then branches across the narrow peninsula through a lovely little glen to ORD on the shore of Loch Eishort, from where there are views across the water to the distant Cuillins.

Facing the mainland, Armadale and ARDVASAR are near the end of the peninsula, the road beyond petering out to a track leading to the Point of Sleat. The wooded landscapes here are in marked contrast to the stark grandeur of the greater part of the island.

Portree–Edinbane, *14 miles*; Portree–Sligachan, *10 miles*; Portree–Broadford, *28 miles*; Broadford–Kyleakin, *8 miles*; Broadford–Armadale, *17 miles*.

Car and passenger ferries: Kyle of Lochalsh–Kyleakin; Mallaig–Armadale; Kyle–Portree. Buses.

County: Inverness-shire.

Hotels   Portree

ROYAL HOTEL (Portree 12). The foremost hotel in the town, centrally placed on the hill facing the sea; well-appointed and efficiently-run; central heating. Bonnie Prince Charlie is said to have stopped here during his flight in 1746. Cabin cruisers available for boating or fishing trips. 53 rooms, many overlooking the sea and all with hot and cold water. Bed and breakfast, 30s.–37s. 6d. Week, 14–17 gn.

COOLIN HILLS HOTEL (Portree 3). In an old house, this excellent hotel has recently been opened by a young couple, who provide modern comfort and food of an unusually high standard. Open all the year. 20 rooms, all with hot and cold water. Bed and breakfast, 30s.–40s. Week, 15–18 gn.

ROSEDALE HOTEL (Portree 31). Small hotel, well-placed among the cottages that line a rocky path along the shore, not far from the steamer pier. Gay and somewhat friendly in atmosphere, with helpful owners. Good food, including fresh lobster. Open May– mid-October. 14 rooms, most with hot and cold water. Bed and breakfast, 21s.–22s. 6d. Week, 10–10½ gn.

Skeabost

SKEABOST HOUSE (Skeabostbridge 202). Luxurious country-house hotel, decorated in perfect taste, with wood panelling, fitted carpets and elegant china and silver. Log fires in the lounge, billiard room. Excellent fishing in the river that flows through the grounds; rough shooting and salmon fishing arranged on the estate. Good food. Open March–October. 17 rooms, each with its own colour scheme and all with hot and cold water. Bed and breakfast, 40s.–50s. Week, £17 10s.–£24 10s.

Edinbane

EDINBANE HOTEL (Edinbane 203). Quietly situated close to the water, this homely hotel seems ideal for a simple holiday. Pleasantly arranged; sun verandah. It has an orchard-cum-garden and supplies its own produce. Sea and river fishing can be arranged. Open May–October. 8 rooms, all with hot and cold water. Bed and breakfast, 21s.–22s. 6d. Week, 11½–12½ gn.

Struan

BALGOWN HOUSE (Struan 202). Simple, pleasing country house in an isolated position, high up with views over the loch. Best for those exploring by car, or who like walking. Cruises and fishing trips arranged, also pony-trekking; excursions to places of interest. Lounge; garden. Unlicensed. 10 rooms, some with hot and cold water. Week, 8½–9½ gn.

Sligachan

SLIGACHAN HOTEL (Sligachan 204). On its own in moorland
country at the head of the loch, with views of sea and hills, this
is a well-known climbers' hotel and also useful for motorists.
Sea trout and salmon fishing for guests; motor-boat excursions.
Lounge, bar, garage. Open Easter–mid-October. 33 rooms (some
on the ground floor) with hot and cold water. Week, 16½–18 gn.

Broadford

DUNOLLIE HOTEL (Broadford 253). Modern hotel on the shore,
with two cheerful lounges overlooking the bay. This would make
a congenial centre for exploring the southern part of Skye.
Climbing and moorland walking; bathing; motor-launch available
to guests for sea trips; also rowing dinghies. The food is excellent
and much care is taken in its preparation and presentation; the
Dolphin Grill is open daily until 11 p.m. Unlicensed. Open
March–end October. 21 rooms, all with hot and cold water. Bed
and breakfast, 22s.–28s. Week, 11–14 gn.

AILEEN COTTAGE (Broadford 278). Small, plain guesthouse on the
main road. Open March–mid-October. 5 rooms, 3 with hot and
cold water. Dinner, bed and breakfast, 27s. 6d. Week, 11 gn.
(without lunch, 8 gn.).

Ord

ORD HOUSE HOTEL, Ord, Isleornsay (Isleornsay 212). This charming small house has a wonderful setting on a slope above Loch
Eishort; remote, amid beautiful scenery, with a panoramic view
of the Cuillins across the water. It is run on personal lines by
two sisters, who provide good home cooking—and whose after-
noon teas are renowned. A safe, sandy beach is below, and near
by are a seal colony, a heronry and a small coral island; boating,
fishing, varied walks. Open March–November. 8 rooms in main
house, 6 in annexe; no running water at present. Bed and breakfast 26s. Week, 10½–11½ gn. Plus 10 per cent service.

Ardvasar

ARDVASAR HOTEL (Ardvasar 223). Agreeable small country inn
with some of the loveliest views on Skye, facing south-east over

76

the sea. Helpful proprietors, who will meet guests at Armadale pier and will advise on excursions. Homely little lounge and sun lounge, cheerful dining-room. Special attention is paid to the food. Open all the year. 8 rooms, with hot and cold water. Bed and breakfast, 23s.–27s. Week, 11–13 gn.

THE FAR NORTH

THE FAR NORTH

JOHN O'GROATS
DUNNET
THURSO   WICK
MELVICH   LYBSTER
BETTYHILL   DUNBEATH
DURNESS   FORSINARD

N

ALTNAHARRA   HELMSDALE

SCOURIE   GOLSPIE
DRUMBEG   INCHNADAMPH   DORNOCH
                LAIRG
Loch Assynt
LOCHINVER
                OYKELL BRIDGE
        ULLAPOOL

AULTBEA   GARVE
POOLEWE   Loch Maree

                .ACHNASHEEN   miles
GAIRLOCH   0   10

Gairloch to Ullapool

The roads to the north-west Highlands, from Strome Ferry to the south and Inverness to the east, meet at Achnasheen. Westwards, the scenery becomes more attractive round Loch Maree, one of the finest in the area.

The little fishing village of GAIRLOCH has a beautiful setting on the sea loch of the same name and has become a holiday centre for those exploring this region of Wester Ross. Loch Maree, Loch Ewe and the Torridon mountains are within reach, and there are sandy bays for bathing round the shores of the Gairloch. The district also offers a 9-hole golf course, and fishing and walking.

Over the moors a few miles to the north is POOLEWE, a fishing centre in rural surroundings at the head of Loch Ewe. On the eastern shore of the loch about a mile from the village, the subtropical gardens of Inverewe House are open daily.

The road climbs out of Poolewe on to rolling moorland, the coast bordered by fields, and through AULTBEA, which overlooks the Isle of Ewe in the loch; then across to outstandingly lovely, utterly unspoilt Gruinard Bay, where there are scattered farms, low-lying granite islands, little landlocked bays with sand and rock beaches, and snowcapped mountains in the distance.

Set on a flat promontory jutting into Loch Broom, the attractive fishing port of ULLAPOOL is a good and well-known holiday centre for the north-west Highlands. All round are wild hills, moors, glens and lochs, with bathing beaches, boating, salmon and trout fishing, pony-trekking, walking and climbing, and excursions by car and coach.

Some 30 miles inland, on the road west from Inverness, where it branches to Gairloch and to Ullapool, GARVE is a convenient stop on the way to or from the west coast.

Edinburgh–Gairloch, *250 miles*; Achnasheen–Gairloch, *29 miles*; Gairloch–Ullapool, *57 miles*; Ullapool–Garve, *33 miles*; Ullapool–Inverness, *61 miles*.

Railway stations: Achnasheen, Garve. Buses; direct summer bus
service Inverness–Ullapool.
County: Ross-shire.

Hotels   Gairloch

GAIRLOCH HOTEL (Gairloch 2). A typical large Scottish stone
house, this high-class hotel stands by the sea just above a little
bay with sand and rocks. Well furnished and well run, with
willing staff; suitable for families. Lift; lounges, bar, games room,
tennis court. Good fishing for guests in lochs and sea; boats
available. Open Easter–October. 53 rooms, all with hot and cold
water, some with bath. Bed and breakfast, 36s.–52s. Day, 48s.–67s.

SHIELDAIG LODGE HOTEL (Badacro 250). This old-style, isolated
lodge stands by the water on a pretty, sheltered inlet of Gairloch,
about a mile from the main road and three miles from Gairloch
village. The surroundings are quiet and lovely and the hotel has
the shooting rights of Shieldaig Forest, as well as free fishing for
guests and tennis court in the grounds. Lounges. Open March–
end October. 17 rooms, all with hot and cold water. Bed and
breakfast, 27s. 6d.–40s. Week, 12–15 gn.

Poolewe

POOLEWE HOTEL (Poolewe 241). On a country road on the edge
of the village, this is a charming small hotel in a fine position
overlooking the loch; the adjoining annexe is equally attractive.
Children and pets welcome. Open all the year. 19 rooms, with
hot and cold water. Bed and breakfast, from 27s. 6d. Week,
14–15 gn.

POOL HOUSE HOTEL (Poolewe 223). Small hotel just off the road
with views over the water. Fishing rights on the River Ewe. Open
all the year. 22 rooms, all with hot and cold water. Bed and
breakfast, from 26s. 6d. Week, 15 gn.

Aultbea

AULTBEA HOTEL (Aultbea 201). Pleasant hotel on the edge of
Loch Ewe. Trout and sea fishing for guests; also bathing, boating

and hill-walking. 21 rooms, all with hot and cold water. Bed and breakfast, 25s. 6d.–26s. 6d. Week, 12–14 gn.

Ullapool

ROYAL HOTEL (Ullapool 8). Well-appointed hotel in a good position at the entrance to the little town, with views over harbour and loch. Lounges, bar. Fishing available. Open all the year. 56 rooms, some newly built and with bath; all with hot and cold water. Bed and breakfast, from 30s. Day, from 48s.

MOREFIELD HOTEL (Ullapool 141). Outside the town, to the west, this hotel stands in its own grounds not far from the loch. It is a large Victorian house with a pleasing atmosphere. Lounge, bar, playroom. Fishing for guests. Open all the year. 20 rooms, all with hot and cold water. Bed and breakfast, 25s.–30s. Week, 14–15 gn.

TIR-ALUIN HOTEL (Ullapool 74). Three miles outside Ullapool, in private grounds bordering Loch Broom. Bathing, boating, fishing in the loch. Unlicensed. Open April–October. 18 rooms, all with hot and cold water, some with bath. Bed and breakfast, from 25s. Week, 13–15 gn.

Garve

STRATHGARVE LODGE (Garve 204). Attractive hotel with the comforts and atmosphere of a private house. The lodge is peacefully situated in its own grounds on a lane outside Garve village. Facilities for sportsmen includes free salmon and trout fishing in Loch Garve and the River Blackwater; also shooting, stalking, sailing. Children welcome. Open from Easter. 20 rooms, all with hot and cold water. Bed and breakfast, 35s.–40s. Week, 18–19 gn.

Lochinver and Scourie

Travelling up the west coast into the far northern county of Sutherland, one drives past small islet-dotted lochs, through open valleys with tumbling rivers and beneath distinctive rocky mountains.

At INCHNADAMPH, at the head of remote Loch Assynt, there are a scattering of attractive whitewashed houses. The lovely road winds on to LOCHINVER, a busy, picturesque small fishing port by the sea, its cottages lining the bay. The village is dominated by the strange, solitary peak of Suilven and surrounded by rugged coast and country.

The narrow coast road from Lochinver climbs and twists between boulder-strewn hills, lochs and rivers and sudden little coves with sandy beaches, such as that at Clashnessie. At DRUMBEG there are splendid views over the rocky coast and islands and the inland hill loch. This is bare and lonely but very majestic country.

About 12 miles north of the Kylesku Ferry (crossing free) is SCOURIE, a remote fishing and crofting village on the wild coast. The climate is mild and the palm trees growing here are said to be the most northerly in the world. There are sandy beaches in the vicinity, good fishing, and a bird sanctuary on the near-by island of Handa.

Inverness–Lochinver, *98 miles*; Ullapool–Lochinver, *37 miles*; Ullapool–Scourie, *45 miles*.

Railway station: Lairg (45 miles). Buses.

County: Sutherland.

Hotels   Inchnadamph

INCHNADAMPH HOTEL, Loch Assynt, by Lairg (Assynt 202). Charming hotel near the loch; for fishermen and those who want walking, solitude and striking scenery. Lounge, bar, garage; car for hire. Free salmon and trout fishing for guests; boats available. 30 rooms, all with hot and cold water. Bed and breakfast, from 25s. Week, £14.

Lochinver

CULAG HOTEL (Lochinver 209). This turreted granite house stands at the end of the bay overlooking the harbour, a comfortable, well-run hotel where attention is paid to serving interesting meals. Salmon and trout fishing for guests; also sea fishing; boats and tackle available. Open Easter–mid-October. 45 rooms, all with hot and cold water. Bed and breakfast, 40s. Week, 18gn.

Drumbeg

DRUMBEG HOTEL, by Lairg (Drumbeg 236). A plain, whitewashed building on the road, this is a fishermen's hotel—modest, with a pleasant, cultivated atmosphere. Good loch and sea fishing free to guests; boats available. Open Easter–end September. 10 rooms, all with hot and cold water. Bed and breakfast, 21s.–25s. Week, from 11 gn.

Scourie

SCOURIE HOTEL (Scourie 6). An old house of character, set among fields, this most agreeable hotel is primarily for anglers, with free salmon and trout fishing; boats available. Also walking, climbing, bird-watching; deer-stalking by arrangement. Open all the year. 19 rooms, all with hot and cold water. Bed and breakfast, 27s. 6d.–30s. Week, 11–14 gn.

Durness to Melvich

Reached across bleak country from SCOURIE, DURNESS is the first village on the far northern coast of Scotland. It is a small, straggling place facing a wild and open sea, with cliffs, headlands and deep horseshoe beaches of golden sand on either side. Across lonely moorland some miles to the west is Cape Wrath, which forms the extreme north-west corner of Britain, while in the cliffs to the east of the village are the Smoo Caves which can be explored by boat.

The coast road skirts the deep sea inlets of Loch Eriboll and Kyle of Tongue. At the pretty village of Tongue one can turn south towards LAIRG across rolling moorland studded with little lochs. At ALTNAHARRA, about 17 miles inland, a deserted second-

ary road along Loch Naver and Strath Naver leads back to the
sea at BETTYHILL. The loch and river Naver and surrounding
waters are known for their excellent salmon and trout fishing.

Bettyhill is a tiny cliff-top village with large, golden sand
beaches below and exposed country behind. Some 14 miles to
the east, MELVICH has sandy bathing beaches, fishing, and views
over cliffs and moorland. Another angling centre is FORSINARD
in the Halladale valley which runs inland from Melvich.

Edinburgh–Durness, *264 miles* (using ferry); Lairg–Durness, *56
miles*; Durness–Melvich, *63 miles*; Melvich–Forsinard, *13 miles*.
Railway stations: Lairg, Forsinard. Buses.
County: Sutherland.

Hotels   Durness

CAPE WRATH HOTEL (Durness 204). Old-fashioned hotel in its own
grounds near the sea loch. A suitable centre for exploring the
district; also good fishing for guests. Lounge, bar. Open all the
year. 20 rooms, some with hot and cold water. Bed and breakfast,
from 22s. 6d. Week, 10–15 gn.

SMOO CAVE HOTEL, Lerin (Durness 227). On the cliffs outside the
village, a modest but acceptable hotel. 15 double rooms, all with
hot and cold water. Bed and breakfast, 18s. 6d.–21s. Week,
8–10 gn.

Altnaharra

ALTNAHARRA HOTEL, by Lairg (Altnaharra 22). A good hotel with
modern amenities, standing off the road in its own grounds.
Dedicated to angling, the hotel has river and loch fishing for
salmon and trout; boats available; angling instruction by arrangement; tackle for sale or hire. Open March 1–October 31. 15
rooms, all with hot and cold water. Bed and breakfast, from
25s. Week, 15–16 gn.

Bettyhill

BETTYHILL HOTEL, by Thurso (Bettyhill 202). Comfortable hotel
on the hill above the beach. Congenial atmosphere; families
welcome. Fishing is the main activity, with salmon and trout in
surrounding lochs available to guests. Open all the year. 17 rooms,

all with hot and cold water; also cottage annexe with 3 rooms and bathroom. Bed and breakfast, 27s. 6d–32s. 6d. Week, 13–16 gn.

Melvich

MELVICH HOTEL, by Thurso (Melvich 206). Granite-built hotel on the hillside above the bay, with sea and country outlook. Salmon and trout fishing by arrangement. 20 rooms, most with hot and cold water. Bed and breakfast, 22s. 6d.–30s. Week, 10–12 gn.

Forsinard

FORSINARD HOTEL (Melvich 221). Sportsmen's hotel set in moorland, providing salmon and trout fishing and shooting for guests. Open all the year. 8 rooms, with hot and cold water. Bed and breakfast, 24s. 6d. Week, from 12 gn.

Thurso and Wick Districts

The bustling fishing town and resort of THURSO is well placed on wide Thurso Bay, and a convenient base for expeditions into this distant corner of the British Isles. At near-by DUNNET a few houses are spread round the large bay, with Dunnet Head, the most northerly point of Britain, rising on one side and a three-mile stretch of sand on the other, dunes and moorland behind.

It is 12 miles on (past the Castle of Mey) to John o'Groats, the north-eastern tip of the mainland. The point is named after a sixteenth-century Dutchman, John de Groot, whose eight-sided house once stood on the site. Gaunt and exposed and overlooking an expanse of turbulent, rock-strewn sea, it is nevertheless a goal for tourists.

Down the east coast, WICK is a strongly-built, grey fishing town with a large and active harbour. At the rather austere village of LYBSTER there are still rugged cliffs, but the character of the landscape changes beyond. Latheronwheel, DUNBEATH and Berriedale are engaging little ports in rocky inlets backed by wooded valleys. Then the road crosses bleak moors and passes the Ord of Caithness, the mountain that marks the boundary with Sutherland.

London–Thurso, *679 miles*; Edinburgh–Thurso, *306 miles*; Thurso–Wick, *21 miles*; Wick–Dunbeath, *22 miles*; John o'Groats –Land's End, *873* miles.

Railway stations: Wick, Thurso, Helmsdale. Airport: Wick. Buses.

County: Caithness.

Hotels

Thurso

ROYAL HOTEL (Thurso 3191/2). Pleasing hotel in the main street about five minutes from a sandy beach. Traditional comfort. Garage. Open all the year. 101 rooms, all with hot and cold water. Bed and breakfast, from 27s. 6d. Week, from 13 gn.

Dunnet

NORTHERN SANDS HOTEL (Castletown 270). Attractive, good-class hotel, set back from the road, with the sands just below. Sea and loch fishing for guests. Lounge with TV; garage. 15 rooms, all with hot and cold water. Bed and breakfast, 27s. 6d. Week, 13 gn.

Wick

MACKAY'S HOTEL (Wick 75). One of the leading hotels in the town. Patronised by businessmen, it is also suitable for overnight stops for tourists. Lounge, bar, TV; garage. Open all the year. 20 rooms, all with hot and cold water. Bed and breakfast, 28s. 6d. Week, 12 gn.

Lybster

PORTLAND ARMS HOTEL (Lybster 208). On the main road, a well-appointed hotel where motorists could conveniently spend the night. Open all the year. 24 rooms, all with hot and cold water. Bed and breakfast, 25s. 6d.–30s. 6d. Week, 12–14 gn.

Dunbeath

DUNBEATH HOTEL (Dunbeath 208). Inviting hotel in a row of gay, terraced cottages among trees, just above the river and road. Free fishing for salmon and trout. About 10 minutes' walk across the fields to the bay. 29 rooms, all with hot and cold water. Bed and breakfast, 25s.–35s. Week, 12–14 gn.

Dornoch Firth and Lairg

Along the east Sutherland coast there is green farming country by the rock and sand shore, with moors rising inland. Both railway and road (one of the few two-lane roads in northern Scotland) follow the sea closely, through picturesque Helmsdale and Brora with its sand beach, golf course and salmon river, to GOLSPIE which overlooks the Dornoch Firth. This pretty resort has a good sandy bathing beach, an 18-hole golf course and fishing, boating and walking. Just outside is Dunrobin Castle, seat of the Duke of Sutherland.

At the mouth of the Dornoch Firth is DORNOCH itself, a historic old town with a cathedral and the remains of the bishop's castle. Today it makes a charming little golfing and seaside resort, with safe sands for bathing and a well-known 18-hole golf course, as well as fishing and hill walking.

About 15 miles inland, the town of LAIRG, at the southern end of Loch Shin, is a centre for the remote far north of Scotland, roads radiating in all directions. It is also an angling centre, as is OYKELL BRIDGE, about 15 miles away on the westward road.

Edinburgh–Dornoch, *238 miles*; Dornoch–Golspie, *12 miles*; Dornoch–Lairg, *21 miles*.

Railway stations: Golspie, Lairg, Bonar Bridge. Buses.

County: Sutherland.

Hotels   Golspie

GOLF LINKS HOTEL (Golspie 287). Delightful hotel in an attractive old house surrounded by a walled garden. It is furnished with taste, and the modern annexe blends with the old part; dining-room with wide windows. Pleasant owners. Adjoining the golf course, with the sandy beach just across the road, it is well suited to golfers as well as to families with children. Boats available for fishing and sea trips. Open all the year. 25 rooms, all with hot and cold water. Week, from 9 gn.

Dornoch

DORNOCH HOTEL (Dornoch 351/2). Rather grand hotel adjoining the golf course and overlooking the beach. Efficiently run and equipped. Lounges, bar; film shows and dancing in summer; putting course and hard tennis court in the grounds. Open May–end September. 85 rooms, all with hot and cold water, a few with bath; some private suites. Bed and breakfast, 37s. 6d.–72s. Week, 18–21 gn. Plus 10 per cent service.

ROYAL GOLF HOTEL (Dornoch 283). Formal hotel in private grounds facing the golf course. Lounges, bar, ballroom. Open March–October. 47 rooms, all with hot and cold water, some with bath. Bed and breakfast, 32s. 6d.–47s. 6d. Week, 14–20 gn.

DORNOCH CASTLE HOTEL (Dornoch 216). In the remaining part of the sixteenth-century bishop's palace, this is an unusual hotel, full of atmosphere—the building contains a "ghost" room, execution room and a passage to the cathedral. Modernised, with tasteful and comfortable décor and furnishings. An agreeable welcome for guests. Lift; bar; pretty, formal garden; garage. Open April–October. 16 rooms, all with hot and cold water. Bed and breakfast, 29s. 6d. Week, 15 gn.

Lairg

SUTHERLAND ARMS HOTEL (Lairg 91). High-class hotel with excellent food and service, in a rambling old house facing the loch. Lounges, bar; garage. Fishing available. Open April–end September. 42 rooms, all with hot and cold water, some with bath. Bed and breakfast, 36s.–52s. Day, 42s.–67s.

Oykell Bridge

OYKELL BRIDGE HOTEL, Oykell Bridge, by Lairg. Pleasing hotel, almost exclusively for fishermen. On the Oykell River, which here forms the boundary between the counties of Sutherland and Ross. Salmon fishing in the river by advance booking with Lower Oykell Fishings, Ardgay, Ross-shire. Open mid-March to mid-October. 7 rooms in hotel, 5 in annexe, all with hot and cold water. Bed and breakfast, 30s. Week, 18 gn.

CENTRAL HIGHLANDS

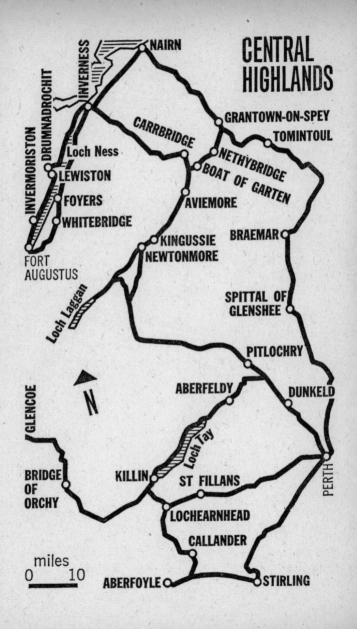

Inverness and Loch Ness

A dignified northern town with an agreeable atmosphere, INVERNESS stands on the River Ness, at the head of the Moray Firth and at the northern end of the Great Glen. It is known as the capital of the Highlands and is an important centre for the whole region.

Sixteen miles away on the sandy shores of the Moray Firth, is the charming little golfing and seaside resort of NAIRN.

Long, narrow Loch Ness runs south-west from Inverness, forming part of the Caledonian Canal through the Great Glen. The waters of the loch are very deep—and both visitors and local residents keep a sharp look-out for the famous monster. The scenery is attractive, wooded hills rising to moorland on either side.

The main road, a busy route to the Western Highlands, follows the western shore. Particularly pleasant is Urquhart Bay, where Glen Urquhart leads into the hills; the ruins of Urquhart Castle stand by the water. Here are the villages of DRUMNADROCHIT and LEWISTON, while a few miles farther on is INVERMORISTON at the foot of Glen Moriston.

The narrow, less-frequented road along the eastern shore of Loch Ness passes through quiet and lovely country. At the village of FOYERS it climbs up on to the moors to WHITEBRIDGE, before descending again to Fort Augustus at the southern end of the loch.

London–Inverness, *549 miles*; Edinburgh–Inverness, *176 miles*; Inverness–Drumnadrochit, *15 miles*; Inverness–Foyers, *19 miles*; Inverness–Nairn, *16 miles*.

Railway stations: Inverness, Nairn. Airport: Inverness. Buses. Counties: Inverness-shire; Nairnshire (Nairn).

Hotels   Inverness

STATION HOTEL (Inverness 31926). This hotel adjoining the railway

GO-ANYWHERE MONEY

GOOD-EVERYWHERE MONEY

Take your pick. Any city. Any country.
Take your pen. ☐ Take your Travellers'
Cheques—from National Commercial. The
secure, convenient way to carry money—
anywhere and everywhere. ☐ Get your
'go-anywhere' Money from any branch of
National Commercial Bank of Scotland.

NATIONAL COMMERCIAL BANK
OF SCOTLAND LIMITED

station is of a very high standard; in the best tradition. Comfortable and spacious with first-class service and good food. It is used as a meeting place by people coming in from the country for miles around, giving an amusing, lively atmosphere. Lounges, bar. Open all the year. 74 rooms, all with hot and cold water, some with bath. Bed and breakfast, from 43s. Day, from 73s. Plus 10 per cent service.

Nairn

NEWTON HOTEL (Nairn 3144). Just outside the town, a dignified house in an attractive park, with views across the lawns and golf course to the sea. Lift; lounges, bar. Open Easter–mid-October. 33 rooms, all with hot and cold water, a few with bath. Bed and breakfast, 35s.–55s. Week, 18–24½ gn.

ALTON BURN HOTEL (Nairn 3325). In a favoured spot on the edge of the town near the sea, a quiet sand and pebble beach only a short walk away across the golf course. Gay, well-kept and friendly, a good choice for families. Lounges, games room, drying-room. Salt-water swimming-pool and tennis court in the grounds. Open mid-March to mid-October. 36 rooms, all with hot and cold water. Bed and breakfast, 30s.–35s. Week, 15–16 gn.

Loch Ness

THE CLANSMAN HOTEL, Brackla (Drumnadrochit 326/7). Modern hotel on the main lochside road between Inverness and Drumnadrochit. Conveniently placed for those touring by car and particularly useful for overnight stops; also used by coach parties. Good views of the loch from the lounge, bar and restaurant; contemporary décor, with tartan much in evidence. Open all the year. 26 rooms, all with hot and cold water. Bed and breakfast, 35s.–40s. Week, 15–16 gn.

LEWISTON ARMS, Lewiston, Drumnadrochit (Drumnadrochit 225). Agreeable old whitewashed coaching inn just off the main road in the village of Lewiston; pretty garden. A good centre for a quiet holiday exploring Loch Ness district; hill walking, fishing. Open all the year. 9 rooms, with hot and cold water. Bed and breakfast, from 30s. Week, 15 gn.

G   97

BORLUM FARM GUEST HOUSE, Lewiston, Drumnadrochit (Drumna-drochit 220). Comfortable, congenial farm guesthouse. In a good position just outside Lewiston village, above the road with views of the loch and hills. Lounge and dining-room have open log fires. Guests sit round one large table for meals, which are plain but good and well cooked, and include home-made bread and butter and Jersey cream from the farm herd. The MacDonald family help to give the place its friendly atmosphere. Families and others with a car could have a very enjoyable stay here; small children will be looked after while families are out on excursions. Pony-trekking daily at £6 a week. Open Easter–October. 6 rooms, all with hot and cold water. Bed and break-fast, 20s.–25s. Week, £10–£18.

GLENMORISTON ARMS HOTEL, Invermoriston (Glenmoriston 206). Attractively whitewashed country inn with pleasing atmosphere and all-round high standard; good food. On the main road where Glen Moriston meets the loch. Bar, garden; garage. Fishing available. Open Easter–end October. 15 rooms, all with hot and cold water. Bed and breakfast, from 38s. Week, 19–22 gn.

FOYERS HOTEL, Foyers (Gorthleck 232). Quiet situation on the hillside with views of the loch; unspoilt surrounding country. The hotel is rather old-fashioned, but homely and comfortable; pleasant proprietor. Salmon and trout fishing; boats available. Open April 1–October 31. 12 rooms, all with hot and cold water. Bed and breakfast, 28s. Week, £12 12s.–£14.

WHITEBRIDGE HOTEL, Whitebridge (Gorthleck 272). On the remote moors above the eastern shore of the loch. Old-fashioned granite house with a garden, by a little river. A fishermen's hotel—salmon and trout. Open May 1–September 30. 12 rooms, all with hot and cold water. Bed and breakfast, 30s. Week, 12 gn.

The Cairngorms

The Cairngorm mountains, which rise to the south of the Spey valley, have some of the highest and loneliest peaks in Scotland. It is beautiful and impressive country.

The main holiday centres for exploring this district are the villages of Speyside, from which summer visitors can enjoy hill walking and climbing, fishing, pony-trekking, and the study of wildlife.

In winter, the Cairngorms are one of the main areas of skiing in Scotland and much time, effort and money have gone into winter sports development, under the auspices of the Scottish Council of Physical Recreation.

The centre of the skiing is Cairngorm Mountain, eight miles from Aviemore, where a specially built road leading into Coire Cas and rising to 2,500 feet, gives access to the main ski run. At the end of the road are a large car park and a shelter and restaurant, The White Lady Shieling, where refreshments are served. The Cairngorm chair-lift takes skiers from here up to nearly 4,000 feet, and there are also rope tows on the slopes and a T-bar tow under construction. Other slopes in the area also.

The winter sports season runs from about December–May, although snow conditions are unpredictable. The Speyside centres and hotels provide all the necessary facilities.

Grantown-on-Spey and Tomintoul

One of the main Speyside centres, GRANTOWN-ON-SPEY is popular all the year. Convenient for touring in summer, it also has good salmon and trout fishing in the Spey and an 18-hole golf course.

In the winter sports season (Christmas to end-April) it is the centre of the Scottish-Norwegian Ski School, with tuition from qualified Norwegian instructors; also curling and skating rink, sports shop, ski hire, dry-ski school, and transport to the main Cairngorm slopes (22 miles away).

Reputedly the highest village in Scotland, TOMINTOUL (1,161 feet) is south-east of Grantown on the southern side of the Cairngorms. It is an angling centre in summer, and in winter there is skiing along the Grantown/Tomintoul/Deeside road.

Inverness–Grantown-on-Spey, *34 miles*; Grantown–Tomintoul, *14 miles*.

Railway station: Grantown-on-Spey. Buses.

Counties: Morayshire (Grantown); Banffshire (Tomintoul).

Hotels   Grantown-on-Spey

PALACE HOTEL (Grantown 7, 207). Modernised and comfortable hotel with a cheerful aspect and central position. Every facility for skiers: hire of equipment, resident instructors, drying-rooms and evening entertainment, including dancing to a 5-man band. In summer there is fishing, golf and tennis, and fishing instruction is available through the hotel. Attractive bar; lounge opening on to the garden. Lift, central heating; garage. Open all the year. 47 rooms, all with hot and cold water, some with bath. Bed and breakfast, 30s.–35s. 6d. Week, 12–17 gn. Plus 10 per cent service.

CRAIGLYNNE HOTEL (Grantown 97). Spacious hotel recently rebuilt, standing in its own grounds overlooking woods and hills. Up-to-date comforts and décor. Games room, dancing, TV, lounges, bar, drying-room, central heating. Resident ski instructors; pony-trekking in summer. Open all the year. 62 rooms, all with hot and cold water, some with bath. Bed and breakfast, from 32s. 6d. Week, from 13 gn.

BEN MHOR HOTEL (Grantown 56). Congenial, comfortable, homely. Lounge, bar, drying facilities, recreation room, central heating. Sports shop and ski-school adjoin the hotel. Open all the year. 27 rooms, all with hot and cold water, a few with bath. Bed and breakfast, 25s.–32s. 6d. Week, 11–14 gn.

Tomintoul

GORDON ARMS HOTEL (Tomintoul 206). Country-style stone house on the village square. Hospitable, with substantial Scottish cooking. Skiers are welcome in winter; instruction available at Christmas and New Year and from mid-March to mid-April. Lounge, bar, recreation room, drying-room, ski-hire. Open all the year. 35 rooms, all with hot and cold water and electric fires, 3 with bath. Week, 10–13 gn.

Carrbridge

A picturesque village on the River Dulnain, a few miles west of Grantown, among woods, lochs and moors.

In winter, CARRBRIDGE is the Scottish-Austrian Ski Village, with two Austrian ski schools, providing instruction, hire of equipment, transport and evening film shows and dancing. The season runs from about mid-December to the end of April. Inverness, *24 miles*; Grantown, *10 miles*; Aviemore, *7 miles*.

Rail. Buses.
County: Inverness-shire.

Hotels

CARRBRIDGE HOTEL (Carrbridge 202). This popular hotel is very much a skiing centre, with a gay, informal country-house atmosphere ideal for young people. In winter there is dancing nightly in the Scandinavian lounge and bar, and a feature of Saturday evenings is the chef's buffet supper; also film shows, table tennis, TV. The Carrbridge Hotel Ski School has six Austrian instructors, and ski shop with equipment for hire. Drying facilities, lounges, central heating; garage. Golf course. Open all the year. 50 rooms, all with hot and cold water and electric fires, some with bath. Day, from 45s. Plus 10 per cent service.

ROWAN LEA HOTEL (Carrbridge 212). Small, homely, informal hotel. Lounge, bar. In winter the facilities of the Carrbridge Hotel

Ski School are available to guests. Open all the year. 10 rooms, all with hot and cold water. Bed and breakfast, 22s. 6d. Week, 11–12 gn. in summer, 14–15 gn. in winter (including ski instruction).

STRUAN HOUSE HOTEL (Carrbridge 242). Friendly hotel, owned by a well-known Austrian ski instructor and his wife. He runs the Carrbridge-Austrian Ski School, and there is a ski shop, equipment for hire, and transport to the slopes. Atmosphere and cooking are both Austrian and Scottish in flavour; evening entertainment includes Scottish dancing, and Austrian music in the bar. Suitable for young people, families welcome. In summer there is fishing, golf and riding in the district, and the hotel is a hill-walking centre. Lounge, garden, garage. Open all the year. 18 rooms, all with hot and cold water, some in the garden annexe. Bed and breakfast, 21s. Week, 9–10 gn. in summer; £15 in winter (including ski instruction and transport).

Nethybridge and Boat of Garten

In a forest, moor and mountain setting on the Spey, NETHY-BRIDGE has a golf course and good salmon and trout fishing. During the winter sports season a team of Swiss ski instructors teaches local visitors; there is equipment on hire, transport to the slopes and evening entertainment.

The village-resort of BOAT OF GARTEN, a few miles beyond, takes its name from the ferry that once crossed the river, now replaced by a bridge. It has an 18-hole golf course, tennis courts, river and loch fishing, and opportunities for walks and excursions.

In winter the ski centre in the village hall provides amenities for skiers from Boat of Garten, Nethybridge and AVIEMORE—tuition by an international team of instructors, hire of equipment, ski shop and store, ski repairs, daily snow reports, transport to the slopes, and entertainments for evenings and bad weather.

Grantown–Nethybridge, *5 miles*; Boat of Garten–Aviemore, *6 miles*.

Railway stations: Boat of Garten, Broomhill. Buses.

County: Inverness-shire.

Hotels   Nethybridge

NETHYBRIDGE HOTEL (Nethybridge 203). Large, comfortable hotel overlooking open country. This is a well-known skiing hotel and is the centre for all winter sports in the village, with instruction, ski-hire, dry-skiing, drying-room. Evening entertainment includes dancing, and during the winter season there is a gay, Continental atmosphere. Lift; lounges, sun lounge, games room, central heating, garden; garage. Angling courses are held during the salmon season in April–May. Open Christmas–October. 74 rooms, all with hot and cold water, some with bath. Bed and breakfast, 30s. 6d.–35s. 6d. Week, 12–16 gn.

GREY HOUSE PRIVATE HOTEL (Nethybridge 216). An attractive old stone house quietly placed off the road just outside the village. Garden, pleasant lounge. Children welcome. Open December 15–October 31. 11 rooms, all with hot and cold water. Bed and breakfast, 20s. 6d. Week, 9½–10½ gn.

Boat of Garten

THE BOAT HOTEL (Boat of Garten 258). Agreeable sportsmen's hotel. In the spring and autumn the hotel has golfing holidays with instruction. Lounges, bar, recreation room, TV, drying-rooms, central heating. Open all the year. 28 rooms, all with hot and cold water and electric fires. Bed and breakfast, 30s.–35s. Week, 13–16 gn.

Aviemore

This popular holiday centre is in beautiful surroundings in the Spey Valley, on the edge of the great Rothiemurchus Forest and of the Glenmore National Forest Park. There are fine views of the Cairngorms, while to the north rise the Monadhliath mountains.

This country offers plenty of walking and climbing, and in winter there is good skiing, since Aviemore is the nearest of the Cairngorm winter sports resorts to the main ski runs and chair-lift, about eight miles away. The Ski School d'Ecosse, open mid-December to May, provides Swiss-trained instructors, hire of equipment and transport.

Inverness, *31 miles*; Grantown, *15 miles*; Pitlochry, *56 miles*.
Rail. Buses.
County: Inverness-shire.

Hotels

CAIRNGORM HOTEL (Aviemore 233). Well-appointed, pleasant if conventional hotel opposite the station and facing the mountains. Skiers catered for in winter, with drying-room, recreation room, and a dance hall that is the centre of entertainment in the village. Lounges, TV, central heating. Open all the year. 29 rooms, all with hot and cold water and electric fires. Bed and breakfast, 30s. Week, 12–14 gn.

RAVENSCRAIG HOTEL (Aviemore 278). Attractive guesthouse just outside the village. Comfortable, with central heating throughout, electric blankets on all beds; log fires and TV; drying-room. Resident ski-instructor. Open all the year. 6 rooms, with hot and cold water, 2 bathrooms. Week: winter, 10 gn.; summer (no lunch), 8 gn.

THE DELL PRIVATE HOTEL, Rothiemurchus (Aviemore 216). Peaceful farmhouse set in wooded country facing the mountains. Outside Aviemore, it is the nearest hotel to the main Cairngorm skiing grounds. Also well suited to families. Open mid-March–end September and at Christmas and New Year. 12 rooms in main house, 6 in annexe, most with hot and cold water. Week, 8–11 gn.

LYNWILG HOTEL, Loch Alvie (Aviemore 207). Country-house hotel on the main road two miles south of Aviemore, overlooking Loch Alvie and the Cairngorms. Lounges, bar, central heating. Open all the year. 14 rooms, all with hot and cold water and electric fires. Bed and breakfast, 26s.–30s. Week, 10–14 gn. Plus 10 per cent service.

Badenoch District

Badenoch is the name given to the upper reaches of the Spey, extending as far as LOCH LAGGAN. Its chief centre is KINGUSSIE, situated on the main Strathspey road, with mountains rising to east and west. Summer walks and excursions; 18-hole golf course; Highland folk museum.

In winter, the Badenoch Ski School based at Kingussie caters for skiers in all the district, including Dalwhinnie, NEWTONMORE, Kincraig and AVIEMORE. There are a team of experienced instructors, a ski shop and ski-hire and repairs; transport is available to the Dalwhinnie and Glen Feshie snowgrounds as well as to Cairngorm mountain.

The attractive village of Newtonmore beneath the Monadhliath Mountains, looks across to the Cairngorms. Pony-trekking is popular here, as well as fishing, hiking and golf.

About 15 miles beyond, on the road to Fort William, Loch Laggan lies in wild country of hills and rocky crags.

Aviemore–Kingussie, *12 miles*; Kingussie–Newtonmore, *3 miles*.
Railway stations: Kingussie, Newtonmore. Buses.
County: Inverness-shire.

Hotels   Kingussie

DUKE OF GORDON HOTEL (Kingussie 302/3). Large hotel with every comfort. Conveniently situated on the main road. Lounges, bar, ballroom. Dressing- and drying-rooms for skiers and anglers. Curling and skating rink, ski instructor, kindergarten for the care of children while parents are skiing. Open all the year. 60 rooms, all with hot and cold water, some with bath. Bed and breakfast, 30s.–35s. Week, 12–14 gn. Plus 10 per cent service.

ROYAL HOTEL (Kingussie 236). Comfortable, conventional hotel. Convenient for winter sports and for climbing and golf; drying facilities. Open all the year. 29 rooms, all with hot and cold water. Bed and breakfast, 22s. 6d.–29s. 6d. Week, 9½–12 gn. Plus 10 per cent service.

Newtonmore

BALAVIL ARMS HOTEL (Newtonmore 220). Small hotel with an informal, hospitable atmosphere and unassuming comfort. Centre for pony-trekking and winter sports. Lounge, bar, central heating, drying-room. Open all the year. 39 rooms, with hot and cold water. Bed and breakfast, 25s.–30s. Week, 9–14 gn.

Loch Laggan

LOCH LAGGAN INN, Kinloch Laggan, Newtonmore (Kinloch Laggan 204). After a fire this isolated country inn overlooking loch and mountains has recently been rebuilt on modern motel lines. The central court has restaurant, lounge and bar, and accommodation for four guests. Set separately on a slope by the hotel's private road are 10 cedar-wood chalets, each with two double and two single rooms and bathroom. Fishing, pony-trekking, hill walking and rock climbing; future activities planned include water-skiing, sailing and shooting. Open all the year. 44 rooms, all with hot and cold water. Bed and breakfast, 30s.–35s. Week, 14–15 gn.

Glenshee and Deeside

More loch, forest and moorland country, typical of the Highlands, spreads to the south of the Cairngorms, much of it reached through Perth, a town strategically placed for those setting out by car, bus or train.

Northwards from Perth, the Blairgowrie road leads on to GLENSHEE and to BRAEMAR, Balmoral and Ballater in "Royal" Deeside.

SPITTAL OF GLENSHEE is a holiday centre in the hills a mile or two below the sharp, steep S-bend known as the Devil's Elbow (altitude about 2,000 feet, often blocked by snow in winter). The road continues over the summit of the Cairnwell Pass and then down to the Dee and Braemar, in a characteristic setting of woods, hills and moors.

In winter, Glenshee is a popular skiing district, especially at weekends. The Glenshee chair-lift takes skiers (and also summer visitors) from a height of 2,100 feet on the main road a mile beyond Devil's Elbow to the summit of Cairnwell mountain at 3,000 feet; the terminal has a car park, shelter and modest cafeteria and there is access to the T-bar and rope tow of the Dundee Ski Club. The Glenshee Ski School, based at Spittal, provides instruction between December and the end of April from an international team of instructors; also ski-hire and repair. In addition there is a sports centre and ski school at Blairgowrie, and on Deeside the Ski School d'Ecosse at Braemar and Ballater. Perth–Spittal of Glenshee, *30 miles*; Perth–Braemar, *59 miles*; Blairgowrie–Spittal, *16 miles*.
Railway stations: Coupar Angus, Ballater. Buses.
Counties: Perthshire (Spittal); Aberdeenshire (Braemar).

Hotels   Glenshee

SPITTAL OF GLENSHEE HOTEL, by Blairgowrie (Glenshee 215). Modern hotel built of wood in Scandinavian style. Particularly suitable for young people and convenient for winter sports. It is the headquarters of the Glenshee Ski School, with resident instructor, ski-hire and ski shop. In summer there is pony-trekking. Accommodation is specially designed for sportsmen and there are drying facilities, ample hot water, heating, etc. In the evenings there are dances and film shows. Open all the year. 17 rooms, most with hot and cold water, some with bath; also some bunkhouse accommodation. Bed and breakfast, 17s. 6d.–40s. Week, 10–16 gn.

DALMUNZIE HOTEL, Glenshee, by Blairgowrie (Glenshee 207). Country-house hotel of charm and character in extensive park and gardens amid the woods and hills of the Grampians, a mile or two from Spittal. Comfort, good food and an agreeable atmosphere. The hotel was originally a shooting lodge, and sporting facilities for guests on the 6,500-acre estate include small golf course, tennis court, shooting, stalking, fishing. Resident ski instructor, transport to the Glenshee slopes (5–6 miles away), and a "snowmaker", which gives guaranteed snow on a nursery slope with ski-tow. Lounges, bar, informal dancing, games room, children's playground. Open all the year. 23 rooms, all with hot and cold water, a few with bath. Bed and breakfast, 30s.–40s. Day, 47s.–57s.

Braemar

INVERCAULD ARMS HOTEL (Braemar 605). Dignified hotel with a baronial flavour; used by the Royal Family. It has an attractive setting overlooking woods and moors. Lounges, bar, TV, games room, central heating. 57 rooms, all with hot and cold water and electric fires, some with bath. Bed and breakfast, from 36s. Week, from 16 gn.

Pitlochry and District

A little grey stone town on the main Perth-Inverness road, PITLOCHRY is a favourite summer resort and a good place from which to explore the Central Highlands. It has a gentle, wooded setting, in the valley of the River Tummel, with moorland rising beyond, the hills purple with heather in late summer. There is salmon fishing, and a fish pass has been constructed at the hydro-electric dam which has formed Loch Faskally on the edge of the town. The Pitlochry Festival Theatre—"Scotland's Theatre in the Hills"—presents a repertory of plays each year between April and October.

There is golf, tennis, boating, pony-trekking and walking, as well as excursions to such places as Loch Tay, Loch Tummel,

Blair Atholl and its castle, the Pass of Killiecrankie and, further afield, Deeside, Speyside, Glencoe, the Trossachs.

To the south-west is ABERFELDY, a small golfing, fishing and walking centre on the banks of the Tay a few miles before it reaches Loch Tay. Also on the Tay, south of Pitlochry on the main Perth road, DUNKELD is a little cathedral city in wooded country.

London–Pitlochry, *462 miles*; Perth–Pitlochry, *27 miles*; Inverness–Pitlochry, *90 miles*; Pitlochry–Dunkeld, *13 miles*; Pitlochry–Aberfeldy, *15 miles*.

Railway stations: Pitlochry, Dunkeld, Aberfeldy. Buses.

County: Perthshire.

Hotels   Pitlochry

McKAY'S HOTEL (Pitlochry 49). Small, family-run hotel; in the main street and therefore likely to be noisy. Comfortable and in contemporary style. Lounge; parking space. No dogs. Open all the year. 17 rooms, all with hot and cold water, central heating. Bed and breakfast, 22s. 6d. Week, from 12 gn. Plus 10 per cent service.

BALROBIN PRIVATE HOTEL (Pitlochry 350). Well-kept hotel in a pretty little garden up on the hill, with a terrace overlooking the valley. It is away from town centre traffic and close to the Festival Theatre. Free car park. Unlicensed. 8 rooms, most with hot and cold water. Bed and breakfast, from 17s. 6d. Week, 9–10 gn.

WELLWOOD HOTEL (Pitlochry 315). A delightful place, set well back from the main road in its own grounds; good food. Open Easter–October. 16 rooms, all with hot and cold water. Dinner, bed and breakfast, 38s.–40s. Week, 12½–14½ gn.

FISHER'S HOTEL (Pitlochry 284/5). Large, good-class hotel in the town centre. Lounges, bar, garden. Open all the year. 70 rooms, all with hot and cold water. Bed and breakfast, 30s. Week, 16 gn.

MOULIN HOTEL, Moulin (Pitlochry 196). Picturesque old coaching inn now an agreeable hotel in the pretty village of Moulin just outside Pitlochry. In addition to the main building there is an annexe with several rooms. Open April–October. 20 rooms, all

with hot and cold water. Bed and breakfast, 27s. 6d.–30s. Week,
13–15 gn.

Aberfeldy

WEEM HOTEL, by Aberfeldy (Aberfeldy 381). Small, whitewashed
hotel, dating back to the sixteenth century and close to the castle
and church of the Clan Menzies, a few minutes' walk from
Aberfeldy. Fishing rights on the Tay. Open Easter–October.
18 rooms, all with hot and cold water. Bed and breakfast,
27s. 6d. Week, 14 gn.

COSHIEVILLE HOTEL, Coshieville, by Aberfeldy (Keltneyburn 219).
About 5 miles from Aberfeldy, not far from the head of Loch
Tay. Agreeable hotel run by a Polish couple. Lounge windows
open on to a verandah and there is a sun lounge. Shooting and
fishing by arrangement. Open all the year. 10 rooms, all with hot
and cold water. Bed and breakfast, 25s.–30s. Week, 12–15 gn.

FORTINGALL HOTEL, Fortingall, by Aberfeldy (Keltneyburn 216).
Excellent small hotel widely known for its good food. Near
Coshieville and Loch Tay. Open all the year. 17 rooms, with hot
and cold water. Bed and breakfast, 28s. 6d. Day, 50s.

Dunkeld

DUNKELD HOUSE HOTEL (Dunkeld 243). High-class hotel in a large,
late nineteenth-century house by the river, approached down a
long drive through the park. Trout and salmon fishing available
to guests. No small children; no dogs. Open March–October.
22 rooms, all with hot and cold water, a few with bath. Bed
and breakfast, from 40s. Week, 16–18 gn.

BIRNAM HOTEL, Birnam, by Dunkeld (Dunkeld 224). Just outside
Dunkeld on the road to Perth. Not very prepossessing in outside
appearance, this hotel has a good reputation and the owner is
anxious to help his guests. Fishing available. 27 rooms, all with
hot and cold water. Bed and breakfast, 32s. 6d. Week, 15 gn.

CARDNEY HOUSE (Butterstone 222). Elegant eighteenth-century
house on a private estate outside Dunkeld, the home of Lieu-
tenant-Commander and Mrs MacGregor, people of character

who provide accommodation for a few guests on country-house party lines; unusual and somewhat exclusive. The house is well preserved and beautifully kept; furnished with antiques and provided with every comfort. Good food. Lift; lounges, central heating. Shooting, fishing and stalking arranged. Open all the year. 21 rooms, some with hot and cold water. Bed and breakfast, 30s.–45s. Week, £15–£20. Plus 10 per cent service.

AMULREE HOTEL, Amulree, by Dunkeld (Amulree 218). Congenial inn, isolated in the hills some nine miles west of Dunkeld. A suitable base for touring by car; also loch fishing for guests; climbing and walking in the district. Lounges, bar. Open all the year. 20 rooms, all with hot and cold water. Bed and breakfast, 30s. Week, 16 gn.

Loch Earn District

Some 30 miles west of Perth, small, wooded Loch Earn offers golf, fishing, walking, climbing, and skiing in winter. At its eastern end is the pleasant little resort of ST FILLANS, and six miles away at the western end, LOCHEARNHEAD. Amid lovely mountains and glens, among them Glen Ogle and Glen Ample— amusing names that tempt one to explore—Lochearnhead is a good touring base, within reasonable motoring distance of the Rob Roy country, the Trossachs, Loch Tay and Glencoe.

A few miles to the north, through grim Glen Ogle, KILLIN is a winter and summer centre at the western extremity of Loch Tay. There is golf and mountain walking and climbing in summer, and in winter Ben Lawers (4,000 feet) provides runs for the skiing enthusiast not seeking mechanisation or organisation. Pitlochry–Killin, *37 miles*; Perth–Lochearnhead, *37 miles*; Killin–Lochearnhead, *8 miles*.

Railway stations: Killin, Balquhidder, Comrie. Buses.
County: Perthshire.

Hotels   St Fillans

FOUR SEASONS HOTEL (St Fillans 276). This is a charming small
hotel on the shores of the loch, overlooking the water. Tastefully
decorated in modern style; lounge, bar. In addition to the bedrooms in the hotel, there are several separate chalets in the
grounds; in the Scandinavian manner, these are well arranged
and equipped, each with double bed-sittingroom, small bedroom
and bathroom. 17 rooms in all. Bed and breakfast, 32s. 6d.–35s.
Week, 16–17 gn.

Lochearnhead

LOCHEARNHEAD HOTEL (Lochearnhead 237). Popular, lively hotel,
with good amenities and service. It would suit families. Sporting
activities organised by the proprietor, himself a keen sportsman.
Swimming-pool and tennis court in the garden; squash court;
sailing and water-skiing on the loch; rough shooting and fishing
for guests; skating and curling in winter. Lounges, bar. Open
December 27–October 31. 60 rooms, all with hot and cold water,
some with bath. Bed and breakfast, 37s. 6d. Week, from 17 gn.

Killin

BRIDGE OF LOCHAY HOTEL (Killin 272). Attractive, rambling white
house on the banks of the River Lochay at the tip of Loch Tay,
just outside Killin. Country-house atmosphere; good Scottish
home cooking. Open March–November. 17 rooms, with hot and
cold water and electric fires. Bed and breakfast, from 30s. Week,
15 gn.

Glencoe District

Approaching GLENCOE from the south, one first reaches BRIDGE
OF ORCHY, in lovely surroundings on Loch Tulla and the River
Orchy. Ancient fir trees here survive from the once extensive
Caledonian Forest. South-westwards, a narrow road follows the

river along delightful, unspoilt Glen Orchy. This area is excellent
for fishing, and in winter the Glencoe skiing is within easy reach.

Glencoe has forbidding but magnificent scenery—deserted
moors, wild green and black mountains and deep, blue lochs—
much of it the property of the National Trust for Scotland. The
village stands on the site of the famous massacre.

The Glen offers climbing and walking, and in winter it is a
popular winter sports area, with skiing at White Corries. The
chair-lift takes skiers from the moor beside the Glencoe road to
the base of the T-bar tows, which rise to about 3,500 feet and
give access to nursery slopes and downhill runs. Swiss ski instruction and ski-hire is provided.

Edinburgh–Bridge of Orchy, *94 miles*; Lochearnhead–Bridge of
Orchy, *28 miles*; Bridge of Orchy–Kinghouse (Glencoe), *17 miles*.
Railway station: Bridge of Orchy.
County: Argyll.

Hotels   Bridge of Orchy

BRIDGE OF ORCHY HOTEL (Tyndrum 208). Up-to-date comfort and
efficient service are provided in this hotel on the banks of the
River Orchy. Good fishing; ski instruction, evening entertainment and free transport to near-by Glencoe during the season.
Large lounge and cocktail lounge overlooking the river. Central
heating. Open all the year. 12 rooms, all with hot and cold water
and electric fires, a few with bath. Bed and breakfast, 25s.–30s.
Week, 13–14 gn.

INVERORAN HOTEL (Tyndrum 220). Isolated in beautiful Highland
country three miles from Bridge of Orchy along a side road, this
would be a perfect place for a rest. The hotel is simple yet comfortable, and the owner is pleasant. Guests return year after year.
Excellent salmon and trout fishing free to guests. Open March–
October. 9 rooms, all with hot and cold water. Bed and breakfast,
25s.–27s. 6d. Week, 12 gn.

Glencoe

KING'S HOUSE HOTEL (Kingshouse 259). Remote in the heart of
the Glencoe mountains, this historic inn (where the Campbells

are said to have gathered before the massacre of Glencoe) has been completely rebuilt and modernised, though keeping its country style, and is now a well-arranged, good-class hotel. Some fishing; well placed for skiing, at the base of the chair-lift. Lounge, bar, TV, drying-room. Open all the year. 12 rooms, all with hot and cold water, electric heaters, radio. Bed and breakfast, 27s. 6d.–35s. Week, 12–16 gn.

The Trossachs

The thickly-wooded Trossachs valley contains three lochs—Katrine, Achray and Vennachar. This very beautiful district of Perthshire has romantic associations with Sir Walter Scott's "The Lady of the Lake" and "Rob Roy".

A few miles to the south and a centre for exploring the Trossachs and Rob Roy country, ABERFOYLE is a small resort near Loch Ard. Another small town convenient for this district is CALLANDER, to the east of Loch Vennachar.

Edinburgh–Aberfoyle, *56 miles*; Perth–Callander, *40 miles*; Aberfoyle–Callander, *11 miles*; Callander–Stirling, *16 miles*.

Railway stations: Callander, Stirling. Steamers on Loch Katrine. Buses.

County: Perthshire.

Hotels   Aberfoyle

FOREST HILLS HOTEL (Kinlochard 217). A hotel of quiet distinction, out in the country beside Loch Ard, looking over the water to hills and moors. Lounge, sun lounge, cocktail bar, terrace, large garden. Fishing available to guests. Children welcome. Open all the year. 45 rooms, all with hot and cold water. Bed and breakfast, from 37s. 6d. Day, from 55s. Plus 10 per cent service.

BAILIE NICOL JARVIE HOTEL (Aberfoyle 202). Agreeable, if rather old-fashioned, hotel on the road between Aberfoyle and Loch Ard. More suitable for overnight stops than a stay of any length.

It is named after a character in "Rob Roy", and a former inn on the site was the scene of an episode in the book. Lounge, garden with putting green. 30 rooms, all with hot and cold water. Bed and breakfast, from 37s. 6d. Week, from 17 gn.

COVENANTERS' INN (Aberfoyle 347). Rustic inn of character, in pretty hill country above the village. A centre for pony-trekking—holidays available at the hotel all through the year (January excepted); also fishing arrangements. Families are particularly welcome, and there are family suites with baby-listening service; also washing and ironing room and facilities for preparing baby food. Lounges, bars, TV, log fires; dancing several times a week. Open all the year. 46 rooms, all with hot and cold water, some with bath. Bed and breakfast, 20s.–30s. Day, 40s.–50s.; inclusive weekly terms for trekking, 14–18 gn.

Callander

BRIDGEND HOUSE HOTEL (Callander 130). Charming old house on the banks of the River Teith with views over the hills; pleasant garden. In the heart of the Rob Roy country and close to the Trossachs. Good cooking—farm produce is used. Open Easter–mid-October. 9 rooms, most with hot and cold water. Bed and breakfast, from 25s. Week, 12–14 gn.

Stirling

STIRLING, an attractive town on a plain, is called "The Gateway to the Highlands" and is a convenient jumping-off point for exploring central Scotland, situated as it is between Highlands and Lowlands.

Stirling has been the scene of many important events in Scottish history, centred round the striking castle on a rock above the town. William Wallace fought the English here, and the Wallace Monument on a hill outside the town gives extensive views. Also

near by is the site of the Battle of Bannockburn, where Robert
the Bruce defeated the English under Edward II.
London, *410 miles*; Edinburgh, *37 miles*; Perth, *35 miles*.
Rail. Buses.
County: Stirlingshire.

Hotel

GOLDEN LION HOTEL (Stirling 5351/4). Leading hotel in the town,
useful for an overnight stop; also a popular local meeting place.
The proprietor is interested in cooking, and the food is good.
Lounge, bar, TV; garage. Open all the year. 90 rooms, all with
hot and cold water, some with bath. Bed and breakfast, from
37s. 6d. Week, 19 gn.

EAST COAST

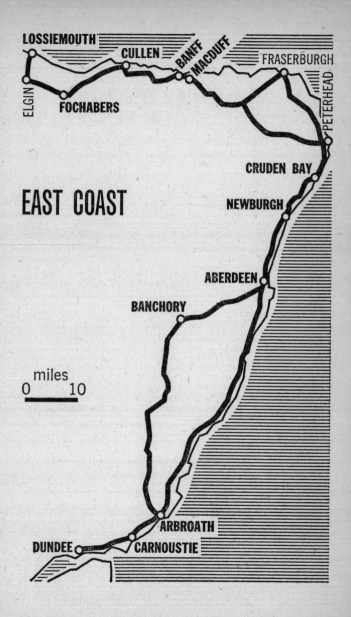

LOSSIEMOUTH
CULLEN
BANFF
MACDUFF
FRASERBURGH
ELGIN
FOCHABERS
PETERHEAD

EAST COAST

CRUDEN BAY

NEWBURGH

ABERDEEN

BANCHORY

miles
0   10

ARBROATH
DUNDEE
CARNOUSTIE

Elgin District

A centre for the Moray area, although not itself a holiday place, Elgin is a distinguished provincial town and royal burgh on the River Lossie a few miles from the coast. There are some grand buildings, among them the ruins of the fine cathedral.

Where the River Lossie meets the sea is the small resort of LOSSIEMOUTH, which has golf, a fine sandy beach—and invigorating air. To the east stretches Spey Bay and the mouth of that famous salmon river, the Spey. Not far away, a short distance inland, FOCHABERS is another convenient stopping-place.

Inverness–Elgin, *38 miles*; Elgin–Lossiemouth, *6 miles*; Lossiemouth–Fochabers, *13 miles*.

Railway station: Elgin. Buses.

County: Morayshire.

Hotels   Lossiemouth

STOTFIELD HOTEL (Lossiemouth 2011). Comfortable hotel on the promenade and opposite the golf course. Open all the year. 44 rooms, all with hot and cold water. Bed and breakfast, from 30s.

Fochabers

GORDON ARMS HOTEL (Fochabers 220). Attractive small roadside hotel. Open all the year. 12 rooms, all with hot and cold water. Bed and breakfast, from 25s. Week, 16 gn.

Banff District

The coast becomes rocky to the east of Spey Bay, but the agreeable small resort of CULLEN has a sand bathing beach and

stands in wooded country; it has an 18-hole golf course. At the
mouth of the River Deveron, BANFF, the county town, also has
sand beach and golf course, and offers good river fishing. Just
across the estuary, MACDUFF has a pretty fishing port on the rocky
shore but no beach. The hinterland is varied and mountains can
be seen in the distance.

Edinburgh–Banff, *185 miles*; Banff–Aberdeen, *46 miles*; Banff–
Cullen, *12 miles*.

Railway stations: Banff, Cullen. Buses.

County: Banffshire.

Hotels
Cullen

CULLEN BAY HOTEL (Cullen 432). Just outside Cullen on the main
coast road towards Elgin, on a hill overlooking the bay, with
the golf course and beach just in front. Lounges, bar, garden,
garage. Open all the year. 24 rooms, all with hot and cold water.
Bed and breakfast, from 27s. 6d. Week, from 13½ gn.

Banff

FIFE ARMS HOTEL (Banff 2427). Good-class hotel, with an engaging
interior, flowers everywhere. Good salmon and trout fishing for
guests (early application advised). Large garden, lounges, garage.
39 rooms, all with hot and cold water. Bed and breakfast, from
37s. 6d. Day, from £2 17s. Plus 10 per cent service.

Macduff

FIFE ARMS HOTEL (Macduff 408). Modest and unexciting, but
acceptable and cheap; on the sea front. Pleasant owner. Glassed-
in verandah on first floor; lounge with TV; garage. 17 rooms,
all with hot and cold water. Bed and breakfast, from 21s. Week,
10 gn.

Cruden Bay, Newburgh

The cliff coast with its little bays and fishing harbours continues
to Fraserburgh, a provincial centre important in the herring

industry. Then the coast turns southwards to Peterhead, another large herring fishing port, built of pink granite.

Some 10 miles down the coast from Peterhead, CRUDEN BAY is a village-resort of some character. It has the long, sandy beach and golf course common to many of the holiday centres in this region. The Bullers of Buchan just to the north provide magnificent cliff scenery.

NEWBURGH is a little grey stone village on the estuary of the River Ythan, known for its excellent sea-trout fishing. There are sand dunes along the shore and opportunities for bathing, golf and the study of wildlife.

Aberdeen–Cruden Bay, *24 miles*; Aberdeen–Newburgh, *14 miles*.
Railway station: Aberdeen. Buses.
County: Aberdeenshire.

Hotels   Cruden Bay

KILMARNOCK ARMS HOTEL (Cruden Bay 213). Pleasing hotel with a pretty garden. Suitable for families; an early evening meal for young children can be provided. Recreation room, billiards, TV. Open all the year. 24 rooms, all with hot and cold water. Bed and breakfast, 27s. 6d.–32s. 6d. Week, 13–16 gn.

Newburgh

UDNY ARMS HOTEL (Newburgh 273). Most inviting, modest family and fishing hotel. The proprietors have the sole fishing rights of the Ythan estuary and will provide information and equipment; drying-room for fishermen; cold store for guests' catches. The hotel is in the village centre, near the river and about 10 minutes from the sea. Electric blankets provided. Open all the year. 18 rooms, all with hot and cold water. Week, 17 gn.

Aberdeen

Where the Rivers Don and Dee meet the sea, the granite city of ABERDEEN has much to interest the visitor and plenty of holiday entertainments.

The granite buildings are each characterised by the different colour of the stone—pink or grey, or the gold of St Machar's Cathedral. The University colleges include: King's, dating from the fifteenth century, and Marischal, an imposing pile, mainly nineteenth-century but going back to the foundation of the college in 1593. Typical, too, are such historic buildings as Provost Ross's House and Provost Skene's House, now a museum.

Modern amenities include a large, well-equipped beach stretching to the north of the town and a golf course to the south; there is an active, interesting harbour and fish market; and excursions can conveniently be made to Deeside and other parts of the area.

On the main Deeside road about 18 miles inland from Aberdeen is BANCHORY, a small country centre suitable for touring. Fishing in the Dee; 18-hole golf course.

London, *515 miles*; Edinburgh, *142 miles*; Peterhead, *32 miles*. Railway stations: Aberdeen, Banchory. Airport: Aberdeen. Buses.

Counties: Aberdeenshire; Kincardineshire (Banchory).

Hotels   Aberdeen

STATION HOTEL (Aberdeen 27214). Leading hotel, with all amenities; modernised. Opposite the railway station and near the harbour, but not too noisy. Open all the year. 62 rooms, all with hot and cold water, some with bath. Bed and breakfast, 43s.–59s. Day, 71s. Plus 10 per cent service.

CALEDONIAN HOTEL, Union Terrace (Aberdeen 29233). Large, good-class, traditional hotel. In a busy part of the city, it is a centre of social life in Aberdeen. Lift; lounges, bar; garage. Open all the year. 65 rooms, all with hot and cold water, some with bath. Bed and breakfast, from 38s. 6d.

EARL'S COURT HOTEL, 96 Queen's Road (Aberdeen 36444). Small hotel set in quiet grounds. Near large Hazlehead Park and on bus routes to city centre and beach. Lounges, bar, parking space. Open all the year. 20 rooms, all with hot and cold water. Bed and breakfast, from 27s. 6d. Week, 11–12 gn.

Banchory

TOR-NA-COILLE HOTEL (Banchory 40). Inviting country-house hotel in wooded grounds. Close to the golf course; shooting and fishing. Lift; lounges, bar, TV. Open all the year. 30 rooms, all with hot and cold water, a few with bath. Bed and breakfast, from 32s. 6d. Week, from 15 gn.

RAVENSWOOD HOTEL (Banchory 282). Family-run hotel, off the main road. Gay and modern, and arranged with taste. Open all the year. 25 rooms, all with hot and cold water. Bed and breakfast, 30s.–35s. Week, 12½–14 gn.

Arbroath, Carnoustie

A picturesque town and port on the Angus coast, ARBROATH has the remains of a fine abbey church and of a medieval castle. There are also sand beaches, an 18-hole golf course and an open-air swimming-pool.

Neighbouring CARNOUSTIE is known primarily for golf, and also has good beaches along the sandy shore and a variety of holiday entertainments.

Aberdeen–Arbroath, *52 miles*; Carnoustie–Dundee, *11 miles*; Arbroath–Carnoustie, *8 miles*.

Railway stations: Arbroath, Carnoustie. Buses.

County: Angus.

Hotels   Arbroath

SEAFORTH HOTEL (Arbroath 2232). Family hotel just outside the town and giving on to the sea. Although the beach is a mile or so away, swimming-pool, tennis courts and other amusements are within 100 yards. Bar, ballroom, TV, garden; garage. Children welcome; cots, special meals, laundry facilities provided. Open all the year. 20 rooms, all with hot and cold water, a few with bath. Bed and breakfast, 27s. 6d.–32s. 6d. Day, 45s.–51s.

Carnoustie

BRUCE HOTEL (Carnoustie 2364). Pleasing, modernised hotel suited to families; children catered for—baby-listening. Excellent food. Situated in a private road about 200 yards from and overlooking the beach and golf course; the railway runs just behind. Lounges, bar, TV, ballroom; garden with two tennis courts; facilities for golfers, including drying-room. Open all the year. 56 rooms, all with hot and cold water, some with bath. Bed and breakfast, 42s. 6d.–80s. Day, 55s.–105s.

Dundee

A busy, compact modern city on the slopes above the north shore of the Firth of Tay, Dundee is one of the leading industrial centres of Scotland. It can be reached from the south across the estuary by car ferry or by the Tay rail bridge; a road bridge is under construction.

Adjoining the town is Broughty Ferry, with its harbour, sands and the sixteenth-century Claypotts Castle. Beyond, towards Carnoustie, you can have the four-mile stretch of Buddon Sands to yourself (but make sure before you go that the shooting range there is not in action). Inland, the beautiful country of the Central Highlands can easily be explored.

Perth, *22 miles*; Aberdeen, *69 miles*; Edinburgh, *66 miles*.

Rail. Buses.

County: Angus.

Hotels

ANGUS HOTEL, Marketgait (Dundee 26874). Recently-opened hotel in the centre of the city. Good-class; modern comforts. Restaurant, TV, lift. Open all the year. 58 rooms, all with hot and cold water and some with bath or shower. Bed and breakfast, from 40s. Plus 10 per cent service.

QUEEN'S HOTEL, Nethergate (Dundee 22515). Well-established hotel, centrally situated with views across the Tay. Restaurant, TV, lift. Open all the year. 48 rooms, all with hot and cold water. Bed and breakfast, from 35s. Plus 10 per cent service.

GENERAL INFORMATION

Scottish Tourist Board,
2 Rutland Place,
West End,
Edinburgh 1.
(Fountainbridge 1561)

For general information and literature on all parts of Scotland. Free pamphlets available; also several useful guides for sale, including "Where to Stay in Scotland", "Scotland for Golf", "Scotland for Fishing".

Literature and advice may also be obtained from the local information office or Town Clerk of main centres.

David MacBrayne Ltd.,
44 Robertson Street,
Glasgow C.2.
(Central 9231)

Local steamer and bus services in the Western Highlands and Islands are largely run by this company, from whom details of timetables, fares, day excursions and inclusive tours are available.

INDEX